Confessions
of an
Introvert

The Shy Girl's Guide to Career, Networking, and Getting the Most Out of Life

meghan wier

SPHINX® PUBLISHING
AN IMPRINT OF SOURCEBOOKS, INC.®
NAPERVILLE, ILLINOIS
www.SphinxLegal.com

Published by Sphinx Publishing, an imprint of Sourcebooks, Inc.
P.O. Box 4410, Naperville, Illinois 60567-4410
(630) 961-3900
Fax: (630) 961-2168
www.sourcebooks.com

Library of Congress Cataloging-in-Publication Data

Wier, Meghan.
  Confessions of an introvert : the shy girl's guide to career, networking, and getting the most out of life / by Meghan Wier.
      p. cm.
  (pbk. : alk. paper) 1. Introverts—Vocational guidance. I. Title.
  HF5382.693.W54 2008
  650.1—dc22
                                2008029909

Printed and bound in the United States of America
BG 10 9 8 7 6 5 4 3 2 1

To my beloved husband: Thank you.
There are no words...

Contents

Confessions
of an
Introvert

Introduction

As an introvert, I can honestly say that I have never been one for the spotlight, and I generally don't crave much attention of any kind. I cringe at the thought of public speaking, and I will avoid phone calls with new people if possible—even if just to order pizza. However, I believe that I have always worked very hard in my professional career, and I do appreciate being recognized for that hard work. The feeling of accomplishment, pride in my work, and the desire to be considered successful drive me to do more and to be more—and sometimes that means doing things that push my comfort level and stretch my boundaries.

After several years of reflection and candid conversations with other people about my own challenges as a business-woman, and later as a business owner, I realized that there are hundreds, if not thousands, of us out there—shy, intro-verted professionals who are trying to triumph in business while balancing the demands of life, family, and convention. I began to examine what it is about me and others that creates the obstacles for career advancement and business success, and to my surprise, much of it came down to inherent personality traits. I hadn't ever labeled myself an introvert, although I certainly knew I was one. But until I took the time to understand the reasons for my own eventual happiness and career success, I was not aware how much the introversion, and my later ability to manage it, had affected my accomplishments.

What I came to know is that, beyond dealing with life's regular idiosyncrasies and injustices, introversion and shyness can be career crippling. Introversion often prevents professionals from establishing strong business relationships, speaking up, proving themselves to others, and being viewed as legitimate and knowledgeable. In some cases, a supervisor or peers may see being an introvert as a weakness—leading to slower promotions and career advancement.

It is no surprise that to be successful, businesspeople need to be heard from and respected. They need to be considered strong leaders and exude confidence. All that is known; however, as introverts, it is natural to seek occasional solitude, feel the drain from interactions with others, and handle social interaction differently. And this is often contradictory to being seen as strong and capable by the people around us. The introvert is at an immediate disadvantage in a business setting, and this can have serious adverse affects. This is what drove me to investigate the habits and skills of other successful introverts and to seek ways to harness that knowledge and share it with others.

I am a shy introvert, but that does not mean that I'm a recluse, socially inept, or unsuccessful in my career. It does not mean that I lack confidence or that I am not a strong leader respected by my peers. It does, however, mean that I have had to use my natural abilities as an introvert. Instinctually I crave time spent alone thinking and preparing. I enjoy the opportunity and excel at working alone, and I have need of fewer, but stronger, relationships than many of my peers. As an introvert, I know I handle social situations differently, and so I use this to adapt my behavior to be the most effective when faced with these types of challenges.

My research and investigation revealed that many successful individuals are introverted, yet they, like me, have learned to project their inner strength outward. As an introvert, this was not a natural process for me but one that evolved through years of first failures and then successes in my professional career.

Being successful is different for everyone, but sincerely considering yourself successful is the greatest accomplishment—the greatest success. For a long time I felt that the goals I sought would not be obtainable for an introvert such as myself. There were just too many factors working against me. What I have come to realize is that I put more roadblocks in my own way than others did. I was the one who could most determine and affect my own level of success. If I wanted it, it may have been hard work, but nothing was impossible. Being an introvert did not stop me from doing anything I hoped to do; it only shaped how I might go about doing it.

The truth is that success takes on many forms. Success is self-determined, it is relative, and it evolves over time. For many years I was essentially a salesperson, and my success was directly measured by the number of sales I made and the dollars I generated. Struggling in this world, I believed that good salespeople were inherently pushy and ruthless—the people around me were being successful at the expense of the clients whom they were meant to serve. I found that type of behavior sometimes unethical and always unsettling and distasteful. I did not want to succumb to that type of behavior in order to meet a sales goal, but I also hated failure. What I did not know, or what I had forgotten in the race for better numbers, was that success cannot always be singularly defined by one goal. I was focused on how many meetings could be set, calls made, deals closed, and yet I still struggled. It was easier to fail, because it is hard to be motivated by more when you derive no pleasure from *any*.

As an introvert, I did not push myself onto others to make the sale. When I tried to follow the sales strategy set by my supervisors and hammered by sales trainers, I fumbled through it, uncomfortable, uninspired, and ineffective. I bristled at the enthusiastic aggression of my peers as they pushed prospects into buying something that they may not have needed or wanted. I was miserable, and needless to say, I wasn't a great salesperson. As much as I wanted to succeed in my job, I never saw myself excelling in sales, because my misconception was that to truly be good, I would have to be aggressive and extroverted like my coworkers. I felt that to be good at sales, I would have to betray a part of myself and become someone I wasn't and did not wish to be. What I later realized was that I had not worked to find a way to have success as an introverted salesperson. Instead, I pretended I was like those around me, just to fail, feel inadequate, and suffer from ever-lessening self-confidence. A similar scenario played out several more times and in several jobs as I looked to find a career that best suited my values, skills, and personality.

In the beginning, I fumbled around, job to job, trying to find a place where I could be confident and successful without losing myself. Perhaps this story sounds familiar to you. In this journey, I have been many things, including a grocery store clerk, a stagehand at a theater, an electrician, a carpenter, a fund-raising coordinator, a salesperson, a sign-shop artist, and a statistical analyst. After a little grounding and direction, I found that I excelled at working on large projects with a variety of people in less structured environments. If I could take the lead and be challenged, I felt more fulfilled, and with each new project, I gained confidence. I began to see that knowing and understanding what life is like as an introvert was an asset. In more recent years, I have been fortunate to have had higher level positions including director of corporate relations, vice president of marketing, vice president of business development, and now as a business consultant and writer. Each of these jobs was very different from the other; taught me a little more about myself, my needs, and my style as an introvert; and strengthened me in different ways. This odd assortment of job titles has given me true perspective on what it means to be successful and how to adapt in different circumstances, and how not to lose myself while thriving in my job (and it does make for an interesting résumé). But best of all, I have had the opportunity to meet, work with, and befriend many incredibly successful but introverted people. While my own story is the one I know best, it is their collective triumphs that drove me to better understand how introverts can and do find high levels of career satisfaction and success.

I once believed that my introversion and desire for intermittent solitude would always be a stumbling block to my success (and in truth, it probably would have been detrimental to my career to hide under my desk on a regular basis). I felt that to be a good businessperson I would have to be outgoing and "on" all of the time. I thought I would have to trade my daily happiness and comfort for a successful, lucrative, fulfilling career. I had even begun to accept that success would never happen on my terms. But as I stubbornly struggled through several careers and incarnations of my outward self, I have been able to find that elusive success—and what it takes to achieve it. More importantly, I have learned how to recognize my own success and to celebrate it.

My current personal definition of success no doubt varies from your own. Over the course of my life journey thus far, my confidence, general happiness, and success have become intertwined and inseparable. One of my first jobs as I was beginning my professional career was working at a theater in development, which meant that I was charged with raising money for the organization. I met daily with the wealthy, respected, and powerful members of my community in order to fund the theater and its programs. As I looked at them, with their beautiful, well-furnished offices, fancy cars, and expensive clothes, I wished so desperately that someday I would be successful like them. But their material things were only physical symbols of their success. These people had become successful because they had overcome their fears, used their strengths, and understood their limitations. I would not have thought any of these people were introverts when I met them. I mistakenly believed this, primarily because they seemed so strong and confident and demanded respect. I too fell into that trap of associating introversion with weakness, and these individuals were anything but weak. But as I got to know these amazing people, I came to learn that many of the rich, powerful, and successful were also introverted—just like me. Yet they had overcome the misconceptions and adapted to reach the high potentials they sought. Many of these people were my secret mentors, and I watched how they conducted business and interacted with others. While I was miserable in my own job, stuck in a position where being shy was considered a flaw, I watched and learned and longed to be like them.

When I finally left that job (and I probably stayed longer than I should have just because I didn't want to sit down with my boss and tell her I was leaving), I took a hard look at myself and my goals. I eventually was able to take what I learned from that job—the characteristics of good (and bad) professionals, mentors, coworkers, and leaders—and determine who I ultimately wanted to be. I wanted to be a leader, someone who overcomes obstacles to reach success. I did not want to miss any opportunity because I was an introvert. But it wasn't until much later that I was able to make this a reality. This first job taught me a lot and exposed me to many wonderful individuals who would not accept that a personality trait like introversion could constrain their success. Fortunately, too, the theater (onstage and front-of-house) is a place where eccentricities are celebrated. While I may not have been an ideal fund-raiser, a few quirky personality traits were generally accepted and appreciated. Today I probably still carry some of my theatrical background with me, and I think that as an introvert, it is good to welcome the occasional bit of whimsy.

Since coming to terms with who I am (an introvert with a rather dry sense of humor and severe workaholic tendencies) and who I wish to be (a respected, successful person who can actually have an articulate conversation with a stranger), I have been able to work toward and achieve many of my goals. In so many ways, the task of success has become more obtainable since I reconciled my strengths and weaknesses, identified areas of improvement, and mapped out my objectives. Of course, I have also come to acknowledge that all of these things change over time and that being successful is a process with no end. Currently, as a small-business owner, writer, consultant, wife, and mother to a young son, I feel that I have reached a certain level of real success, but I have no desire to stop here. There is so much more to be had, to learn, and to accomplish. My success story, and yours, is still evolving.

shy girl tip:

Making the Most of Activities

There are several activities throughout this book. You may want to get a clean spiral notebook or start a computer file for your work. These activities are meant to show you areas of improvement, opportunities for success, and strategies to achieve them.

My intention in writing this book is to share with you what I have learned, a little about my story, and ways that you can use my struggles to learn how you too can be happier, more fulfilled, and more successful (however you wish to define your own success). Much of the information I share is directly related to success for introverts, but there is also some general advice that was generated as I sought ways to cope or overcome the situations that my introversion had created. I hope that you take away a lot from this book, but most of all I want you to remember that success and achievement are self-determined. Once your ambitions and aspirations are identified, your own journey can begin as well.

Chapter 1

So Am I an Introvert (or Just Kind of Shy)?

− ACTIVITY −

QUIZ: ARE YOU AN INTROVERT?

Please answer the following questions, thinking about your most common reaction to these situations.

1. You are at a party alone, and you are having fun but must leave to get home before it gets too late. Do you…

A. Grab your coat and sneak out quickly, happy for the quiet solitude of your car.

B. Seek out the host, give him or her a quick hug, and

say your good-byes standing at the door a few minutes but feel relieved when you finally slip into your bed—you are exhausted!

C. Loudly announce to the whole party that you have to go, waving and shaking hands and hugging everyone all the way to door. You don't want to leave and put it off as long as possible.

2. You give a presentation at a large business conference sponsored by your company. You are confident that it went well. Afterward you...

A. Put your head down and then sprint for the nearest exit and go back to your office.

B. Grab one of your close coworkers to go out for coffee and talk about the event or to go for a walk.

C. Tell the crowd that you will stay for thirty minutes to answer questions, and then end up talking to people until the janitor kicks you out of the room.

3. You and your spouse are planning a vacation. Do you...

A. Ask if you can just take the week at home to catch up on your reading. Your ideal vacation is spent not talking to anyone.

B. Suggest renting a secluded ocean condo for the week with a couple of friends or family members. Your ideal vacation is one that is quiet, one that you can use to rejuvenate yourself and enjoy time with a few close companions.

C. Start looking up adventure vacations and party cruises on the Internet. You want to let loose and enjoy a ton of new people and all the festivities.

4. You have a tough review at work. You are really nervous, but in the end you are given a decent raise. When you arrive home you…

A. Feel happy about the outcome but keep the news to yourself—you don't feel the need to let everyone know what is going on in your life.

B. Decide to take a nap before dinner—the review was tiring! But then you call your best friend that evening to share the good news.

C. Go home? No way! You take all of your coworkers out for drinks to celebrate your good fortune.

5. Your New Year's resolution is to lose ten pounds, so you decide to get a gym membership. Do you...

A. Change your schedule or wake up extra early so that you can go work out when the place is least crowded.

B. Dig out your headphones so that you can listen to your music and avoid conversations with strangers while on the treadmill—you need the time to yourself even if you're surrounded by others.

C. Immediately head for the aerobics class so that you can be with a room of people—you know that the group will motivate you to do more.

If your answers are...

Mostly As: You are *shy*. You may have a hard time making new friends and connecting with others. You will probably never be called the life of the party. You may not feel like you know yourself yet, and you don't feel like you have many friends. You hate opening up and feel awkward when asked about yourself.

Mostly *B*s: You are an *introvert*. You require time to recharge after meetings, parties, or time with new people. You might be shy or may consider yourself social, and even enjoy large events, but you won't be leading the group for the after-party celebration. You would rather go home and unwind alone. You protect your personal time with a vengeance, and you seek out friends who understand that you need occasional time away. You excel at building strong personal relationships with a small group of close friends—because you value these people immensely.

Mostly *C*s: You are an *extrovert*. You are the person who bounces around the party meeting and greeting and loving every moment. After the big event or meeting with a new group of people, you are invigorated and enjoy the high, and you will be disappointed or sad when it is all over. You spend "alone time" trying to find someone to talk to—you almost always want to be with others. You are popular, your list of friends is a mile long, and you crave adding to it.

"Mommy, she's *embarrassing* me! Make her stop, *pleeeze!*" I sobbed in desperation. My pregnant mother, who was crammed awkwardly with two little girls in a tiny public bathroom stall, looked at me unsympathetically. "Meghan, she's two, she isn't going to stop." My little sister, crouched down on the floor, head popped into the next stall, was pleasantly chatting with the nice lady who had the misfortune of being trapped in the stall next to us. I wanted to disappear. My sister had absolutely no problem making new friends and talking to strangers, even at two years old. But to me, having someone's unexpected attention—especially unwanted and unsolicited attention—was beyond mortifying.

I was five when that bathroom incident took place, and it was the first time I can remember being aware of my own self-consciousness. My sister's casual approach to making new friends was so foreign to me that even being in her presence while she gleefully introduced herself to anyone who would listen was difficult to accept. This awareness of self, the desire to focus inward, and the discomfort I felt with new people are what characterize me as an introvert, but self-awareness is also one of the things that gives me the strength and motivation to succeed today.

So many times in my life I was presented with situations in which I wanted to disappear, to become invisible. Social events, family gatherings, and average school days were at best uncomfortable for me, even physically difficult, and over time I developed a habit in these situations of sneaking off to a quiet place to regroup, gain composure, and recharge. I grew up with people excusing my antisocial behavior with comments such as, "Oh, she's just shy." But being shy is more about being timid, easily frightened, and tentative in committing oneself. Shyness and introversion often go hand in hand, but they are not the same thing. I can be shy on occasion, but that wasn't why I preferred sitting alone, reading a book, grabbing a drink with just a single friend, or curling up on the couch watching television on a Friday night instead of being out at the clubs with groups of my classmates in college. I like to have time and space to think and be alone. And I have never liked crowds of strangers (or making friends in public bathrooms), because I find it exhausting, and that, in its simplest form, is what makes me an introvert.

An introvert seeks time to spend in quiet, cerebral pursuits. This doesn't necessarily make him or her brainy; rather, the introverted person by his or her very nature has more time to get to know him- or herself. After all, introverts spend the most time studying what makes them happy, contented, or different. They develop an acute self-consciousness and self-awareness— and these qualities are wonderful gifts for introverts. The truth is that our society caters to the extrovert, so any advantage that an introvert can get and recognize is of benefit, but these gifts are the differentiators that allow the introvert to excel in situations where thought and processing information on a deeper level is tantamount. Introverts can be found in truly every profession, but you would be hard pressed to not find them in research labs or programming away in dark cubicles in software companies. Introverts are generally drawn to professions that allow them to be most comfortable, and good at what they do, alone.

As much as I like being alone, I can be a pretty friendly person given the right circumstances. I always thought it was strange that in some situations I could be social but in others I was very antisocial. I was confusing shyness with being an introvert, and as I got older, I have also become less shy. While I don't believe that one can ever "get over" being an introvert, I do believe that shyness can be overcome. Admittedly, now there are times when I do like to be the center of attention, but at other times I would rather not be noticed at all. I have learned that it is common for many introverts to have a social side and a nonsocial side. In the book *The Introvert Advantage*, Dr. Marti Laney explains that introverted public figures are driven to center stage for different reasons than extroverts are—it is the introverts' passion for their work that draws them to the unlikely profession rather than the desire for the attention. Dr. Laney's book confirmed that my exhaustion after giving a speech or going to a party is very common for introverts, even for the ones who feel natural and comfortable in social situations.

So, what if you don't want to limit your career because of a personality trait? You don't have to. One of the intrinsic elements of introversion that is most significant for businesspeople is that meeting new people is exhausting. I can be social, especially with a group of close friends, but afterward I need some solitude to feel like myself again. While my extroverted friends are able to gain energy from all of the new people they meet, I find it both physically and emotionally draining. I generally avoid unfamiliar social gatherings, except under very specific conditions. This, combined with a reluctance to speak up, was a professional disadvantage. Perhaps the same is true for you. However, I have worked hard to become the kind of self-assured person who stands up and is heard. I evolved into a less shy person over time as a career survival technique. My business success dictated it—and yours may too. For me, it was a long process—something that took time—but eventually I learned how not to be the shy girl. You too can discover the simple acts of making eye contact, holding your head up high, and holding someone in a smile. Shyness dissipates as you gain confidence, and the transition is profoundly empowering. Introversion, by contrast, is something that stays with the introvert for a lifetime. However, there are techniques that you can adapt to a professional setting and find that success you seek. While I will always be an introvert, I am comfortable that there is nothing wrong with that. I can be an introvert, manage my outward personality and presentation, overcome my shyness, and feel content in my environment in order to be the most effective, and so can you. Knowing who you are and what you need are the tools that will allow you to achieve success in all areas of your life.

I have been asked dozens of times what the difference is between introverts and extroverts, the whys of introvert behavior, including why it isn't something we can fully change or get over. The way I usually explain this is that

introverts are drained of energy after an especially difficult situation—as anyone is. Except for the introvert, these
difficult situations can be something that extroverts see as
merely simple interactions with other people. Think of the
last time you had a rush of adrenaline—perhaps when you
were frightened by a loud noise or a near-miss car accident.
Afterward you felt your heart pumping and your body going
limp and weak; you may have felt sick to your stomach. You
were exhausted and physically drained. And that feeling is
miserable. Introverts have this same physical rush of adrenaline that pushes them through the party, speech, or meeting.
It is a fight-or-flight response, and it may even happen before
the event starts. While in most situations this is probably not
as intense as the feeling one would get if he or she crashed a
car, the end result is the same—that physical energy drain.

By contrast, having spoken to many extroverts about
their own physical reactions to similar group gatherings,
extroverts often report feelings of euphoria. They cannot
understand why anyone would not find the experience
purely enjoyable. Parties or events for an extrovert are
a rush—fueled by endorphins. Extroverts, too, have a
chemical response like introverts, only theirs is profoundly
different. They even get addicted to that euphoric feeling,
which is why there will always be someone who doesn't
want the party to end, even after you have long since
escaped out the door and are headed to the comfort of
your home.

There are obviously varying degrees of introversion, and all introverts react more or less introvertedly in different situations. However, there are several personality traits that tend to be most associated with introverts, such as the need to be alone sometimes; a quieter, more thoughtful approach to difficult situations; and the mental and physical exhaustion subsequent to an event or exposure to a group of people.

At the end of this chapter, you will find a brief breakdown of more differences between introverts and extroverts. Since you picked up this book, though, you probably identify yourself as an introvert and have more of the introvert-like qualities. This book will assist you in separating your shy traits from introverted ones, in managing difficult public situations, in determining your introvert style, and in acknowledging your strengths. You may also be able to better determine the introversion or extroversion of those around you. Through this process you will be able to build your personal network, grow your business sense, find fulfillment in your career and community, and more readily connect with the people around you.

The perceived negatives associated with being an introvert can be managed by the same thoughtfulness and self-awareness that makes someone an introvert in the first place. With careful self-examination and time, introverted behavior can be managed and even leveraged for significant personal and professional gains. I have found that being an introvert—even a shy introvert with stage fright and a bit of social anxiety—is in fact, a gift; it is what makes me me and allows me to excel in different ways. While I may know many people in my community and beyond, I still often avoid group situations when given the opportunity, which I have come to learn is OK. True liberation and relief came for me when I realized that there isn't anything wrong with this behavior or with me. What this means is that the people with whom I do socialize and bring into my life are very special, thoughtful, friendly, interesting, giving, intelligent, patient, and profoundly wonderful. I bring them into my inner circle because they are good people who support my business and support me. They will be honest with me, and they wish to see me succeed. They each bring me something unique, and I am able to give them something unique in return.

In recent years I have seen many of my clients who are very smart, dedicated, deserving businesspeople struggle with their shyness and introversion. Over and over again, these hardworking, brilliant people look for ways to succeed, break the mold, and make a difference. Yet they are anxious about marketing, business networking, cold-calling, presentations, meetings, and hiring the right people—each of which is critical to business success! They become miserable, frustrated, and unable to get to the next step. I wrote this book for them, and for all of you who find yourselves in similar situations, knowing that you have the ability to be great and to make a difference but are unable to manage the introversion that is holding you back.

– ACTIVITY –
INTROVERTS VS. EXTROVERTS

Review the list below to learn about some of the different qualities of introverts and extroverts. Are you more introverted or extroverted?

Introverts	*Extroverts*
• seek occasional solitude	• seek out social situations
• avoid interaction with new people	• enjoy interaction with new people
• are excellent listeners	• are excellent talkers
• prefer a small, close group of friends	• prefer a large social circle
• keep thoughts to themselves	• speak their minds
• conserve personal energy	• expend personal energy
• feel weak or tired after an an event	• feel invigorated after an event

REACHING OUT AND REACHING IN

Even as an introvert, I have always wanted to share what I have learned with others. But besides wanting to impart my newfound knowledge and expertise, I also have a profound passion for seeing others succeed. I glean my own personal success from the success gained by those around me.

As a businessperson, one of the best lessons you can learn—especially if you are an introvert—is that in business you cannot succeed on your own. Introverts sometimes forget to reach within themselves for the personal strength to reach out to others. We must make and nurture connections with the people around us to be successful ourselves. Our success would be worthless if there was no one there to observe, benefit from, and in turn succeed. Share your knowledge and expertise, and seek out the same from others—make connections, reach in, and reach out.

GETTING WHAT YOU WANT OUT OF LIFE

"What do you want out of life?" is a hard question to answer. However, in order to get what you want, you have to know what you want. As an introvert, you may have to fight harder to get there—so it is important to have a clearly defined goal or set of goals. You may already be perceived as weak or ineffectual in your job, so establishing these goals can assist in showing your drive and ambition. Besides creating a road map to get to your destination, having the goal will allow you to push through fears and anxiety, challenges and failures. Universally, introverts fear something, and that trepidation holds them back. I find that by defining my goal, I focus less on what might make me uncomfortable and more on my passion for success. Have you recently thought about who you want to be, and what you wish for your life? Has it changed from what you thought you wanted when you were younger?

The following is a four-step process for getting the most out of life. It is a simplistic approach to a complex question, but it will help you to articulate what you want the most and to start developing your personal plan to get you there.

– ACTIVITY –
WHAT DO YOU WANT OUT OF YOUR LIFE?

List and answer the following questions at the beginning of your notebook to help you figure out what you want the most out of your life.

1. Write down your priorities. What are the things in your life that make you the happiest, feel the most fulfilled, and have the greatest impact? Are these the things that you are doing or working toward? Consider all aspects, including family, career advancement, and finances. These should be your priorities in life—the foundation from which you will be building—and the things you should be working toward every day.

Please give this some time and reflection, and don't limit yourself on the basis of your feelings about what an introvert should do or be.

2. Plan and execute changes. Once you have developed your priorities, begin to determine the best way to give those things the respect they deserve with your attention, dedication, and hard work. This strategy may take time and needs to be accomplished in steps. If you want to be able to spend more time with your family, think about the ways you could accomplish this. Is taking a part-time or flextime position possible? Will you be able to work one day a week or month from home? Can you take a pay cut, or do you need to make more money to maintain your standard of living? What tasks must you complete to meet your goals, and what is your timeline for accomplishing each step? Who do you need to talk to, and what do you need to do to make this happen? Perhaps this is a one-year goal or a five-year goal. Put time horizons on these goals, and write down each task required to meet your priorities and accomplish your goals. Think about ways to manage these tasks in a way that you, an introvert, will be comfortable with but that will still challenge you.

3. Develop a personal mission statement. From your responses to the first two steps, develop a mission statement about how you want to behave, how you want to be perceived, and what you wish to accomplish. For example, write: "To strengthen personal relationships and spend more time with family while growing my at-home business to a successful, sustaining, marketable enterprise in the next twenty-four months."

4. Connect with others. Establish, develop, and cultivate relationships with people in your life with similar values, priorities, and work ethics. Introverts rarely think of this as a priority because it seems unnatural or too time consuming. They fear rejection or feel awkward and exposed. Yet the payoff is great. We can accomplish very few goals in our lives solely on our own. Consider and list the people in your life with whom you wish you were closer—friends, family, coworkers, or acquaintances—and make time every day to spend building relationships. If it helps to do so, dedicate an hour each day in the morning to calls, email, and meetings. Make connection a priority. Work to make these relationships assist you in meeting your goals. During your time together, work toward feeling comfortable enough to share your goals and priorities, and learn what works to make each experience better.

Last year, a client of mine—who had identified herself as an introvert—had the goal to quit her full-time job as a corporate recruiter and start a home-based business so that she could spend more time with her two young children and eventually open a retail store. While she liked her job and had accomplished much, she felt that this was a great time in her career to take time away from the corporate setting and pursue an entrepreneurial calling. She and I were sitting down and chatting one day about where she saw her career going when she shared her goal with me. I felt honored to be able to be a part of her journey, and of course I gave her my support in the transition. Through a series of conversations over the course of the next month, I asked my client to identify what she had to do to prepare herself—saving enough money for her initial investment, researching other successful businesses, creating a business plan, making contacts, and taking online business courses. Some of these steps were more difficult for her because, as an introverted person, she knew she would have to extend herself to new people, potential clients, and contacts in a way she had not before. She had many fears, yet because she was passionate about accomplishing her goal, she made a priority of networking, building strong relationships, and focusing on high-value activities. When she finally quit her job and filed the paperwork for her new business, she had the support system and client base already in place. Today she is happily running her successful business from her home, having replaced her previous salary and then some, with plans to open a retail store within the next two years. But best of all, she is able to be with her family more, which was her biggest goal.

Happiness, success, reaching your goals—you need to identify and break down these things to accomplish them. Think of it as a road map. As you begin to piece together and plan the details of your own road map to success, just as my former client did, keep in mind the things you want out of life and understand that although what you want today may differ from what you want tomorrow, that is no reason not to start down the road today.

THE RULE OF PERSISTENCE

Anyone who has ever learned how to ride a bicycle as a child knows that success does not usually come on the first try. Practice, hard work, and persistence are all integral elements of long-term gain. As an introvert, it may be easy to convince yourself that your persistence won't pay off because you aren't being listened to or don't have the charisma to get people to listen. Persistence and passion go hand in hand, and just as your parents told you when you were six years old and learning to ride that bike, just keep trying.

Many years ago, I had been at a job for more than two years when my supervisor left for a new opportunity. I had convinced

---

shy girl tip:

Being Persistent

Post a reminder to yourself somewhere where you will see it every day. A little note in your car, on your television, or on your desk will keep you reminded of your goal and motivate you to be persistent.

myself that I would be promoted to her position. I was overwhelmingly disappointed when my colleague who had started a year after me (whom I had trained) was promoted and then became my boss. The primary difference between my colleague and me was that from the moment she started the job, she made it known that she wanted the higher position. She met with management on a regular basis to discuss how she could improve and talk about her accomplishments and what she needed to do to be ready for the promotion. Meanwhile I quietly waited, thinking that my seniority and hard work would pay off. She was persistent. I was passive.

I learned my lesson.

Since then, the more that I have wanted something, the more passionate I was about it, the more persistent I have been. To be a success you need to have persistence of drive, persistence of vision, and persistence of action. You will be doing yourself a disservice by not staying resilient. If you want the promotion, ask for it. If you need a business contact, seek it. You need to expect that on your way to success there will be trial and error and challenges along the way. Your persistence will allow you to learn from these challenges and break through to that next level.

Persistence always pays off. For me it meant that I fought my instincts to keep my head down, and I too let my supervisors know that I was interested in and ready for a promotion. I showed my passion for advancement and leadership, and the next time a position was available, I got the job.

– ACTIVITY –
PERSISTENCE

How can you be more persistent in your career now? Remember that the key to persistence is passion. Are you passionate about your career goals, and do you show it? Can you see ways to work toward your goals in a more proactive way? Have you been passive and missed out on an excellent opportunity? Have you ever not applied for a promotion, not asked someone out on a date, or not gone to a networking event, thereby missing the chance to grow your contact base or further your career?

Take your notebook and draw a line down the center of a new page. On the left side, write that missed opportunity at the top of the paper and answer the following questions below it:

1. Why did you not pursue an opportunity to its fullest? Were you scared, intimidated, too busy? Did you fear rejection or the way it would make you "look"?

2. How do you feel knowing that you could have changed the outcome of that situation? Angry, disappointed, frustrated?

3. What did you learn from this situation?

4. Did you do everything that you could have done? Did you show your passion, make it a priority, and stretch outside your comfort zone to make this opportunity a reality?

5. Most of all, did you believe in the value of this goal?

On the right side of the paper at the top write down the following:

1. A goal you have for the next month, such as to lose five pounds, to organize your contact list, or to close a sale.

2. What are the hurdles to accomplishing this goal? Fear, time, confidence?

3. Using what you learned from the situation in the left-hand column, write down how you will handle this situation differently.

4. Will you do whatever it takes to make this goal happen, even if it means a sacrifice of some kind?

5. Do you believe that this goal is worthy of your time, your effort, and the risk?

Look back at the left-hand column. Are the reasons you were unable to reach your opportunity the same ones that you see as your hurdles today? What can you do to use your persistence, your passion, to succeed in this goal?

If you need more time, prioritize, delegate, and eliminate the less valuable activities. If you are fearful, find ways to take away the power it has over you. Remember that you can overcome anything with persistence.

EMERGING FROM THE SHADOWS

Growing up, I was not a standout in school, music, or sports. I was not tall or short, ugly or beautiful. I had no great talent for athletics, music, or art. I easily slipped just below the radar, neither liked nor disliked by my peers, teachers, or neighbors. I was essentially invisible. And to be honest, I liked it that way. It suited me. Of course, then I grew up, entered the workforce, and discovered that I was still invisible. And I no longer liked being invisible.

Being invisible in business and in life is a sure way to be forgotten. I began to realize the effects of my invisibility—

not being recognized for awards or being congratulated on a job well done, and then later being passed over for promotions. I began to resent my mediocrity. While being invisible in high school and college had allowed me to float through unnoticed, unflustered, and unhurt, it also had failed to prepare me for a professional career in which those who are noticed advance and excel. I had allowed myself to become essentially invisible to my supervisors, thus missing potential leadership roles or consideration for new projects. I had to acknowledge that I had always secretly longed to be noticed, admired, and respected. I wanted to be a success—and I wanted others to recognize my hard work and expertise. Not only was there the desire for greatness, but also for financial gain. With promotions come raises and bonuses, and a life that I wanted to lead.

Wanting and deserving success are made a thousand times more difficult for the introvert. Situations that others may readily seek, such as being invited to a company lunch or being given public recognition, I purposely steered clear of. The idea of being singled out or having to be social in a new environment caused physical discomfort and was stressful and overwhelming. It wasn't until I was finally promoted for the first time that I saw how to become visible. I had set a goal and pursued it with persistence. I acknowledged my worth to myself and saw value in stretching outside of a comfort zone. It was the first taste of recognition for improvement and leadership, and it fed my desire to fight for my goals.

I no longer had to be invisible. Neither do you.

SHYNESS, SOCIAL ANXIETY, AND STAGE FRIGHT—OH MY

I am, like many introverts, riddled with three other related social problems: shyness, social anxiety, and stage fright. While others may have trouble giving a speech or talking to new people, I have a challenging combination of factors that could have held me back or that I could have used as excuses. And they did hold me back for quite a while. Yet I have, on the whole, excelled at each of my careers—at least eventually!

During school, my days were often spent trying to blend in and disappear. I didn't want to draw attention to myself in any way. The idea of speaking in front of the class or giving a presentation was so overwhelming to me that my heart raced, my head throbbed, and I visibly shook from head to toe. I probably lost every spelling bee I was ever in, not because I couldn't spell but because I could not stand in front of a group of people and pull it together enough to show anyone I could spell. I avoided confrontation and conversation, and I tried to find ways to interact as little as possible.

As the years went by, I had to admit to myself that there were numerous times in my life that being a little more like an extrovert and a little less shy would have allowed me further success—or at least the opportunity to reach my real potential. Being in a school play, club, or competition might have been fun and taught me something valuable. I slowly began to realize that I was robbing myself of opportunities because I was scared to take that step outside of my comfort zone and go after them.

The world does not come to a crashing halt if you take a chance, if you embarrass yourself, or if you talk to a new person. The only thing that happens is that life goes on. My biggest obstacle in managing my own shyness was the fear of looking silly, stupid, or out of place—and this is very common among introverts. For some reason, the idea of looking bad weighs on us and clouds our judgment. I feared looking silly, and yet I realized that standing in a room full of happy people at a party all by myself in a corner was silly and stupid and out of place. For me, being the kind of person who doesn't take a little risk in life was quite possibly the riskiest thing of all.

Even worse, what is the point of going to a party and spending the time alone? I could be happily sitting with a few of my friends drinking margaritas on my porch getting to know one another better or talking to one of my incredible sisters on the phone. My point is that if large group situations make you uncomfortable and will never be your thing, don't do large group situations unless absolutely necessary. There will be times—such as your best friend's wedding or a company holiday party—when you will need to be present. When you find yourself unable to gracefully bow out of these situations, remember the things that help you cope, such as sitting toward the outside of the large group or disappearing for a few minutes on your own to take a short walk in the middle of the event. Plan for time alone afterward and focus your attention on the reason you are at the function in the first place.

For the most part, you can control how the world sees, relates, and interacts with you, and there is no rule that says you must attend every large gathering you are invited to. A striking example of this for me was an open networking happy hour put on by a local technology group that meets every month. This is one of the kind of events that my peers spoke of with enthusiasm and regularly pleaded with me to go. Well, needless to say, my instinct was right on this one. I had dreaded going because of the sheer volume of people, but upon my arrival I realized both why my peers enjoyed it and why I would not. The event took place in a crowded, noisy bar.

To me, there is not much that is worse than awkward conversation with inebriated strangers. This type of event was never going to work for me—and I decided my time was better spent in other networking venues.

Your time is too precious for you to be miserable, and if you cannot manage in a crowded environment, spend your energy excelling in environments where you can success-fully function. Find the social situation that will work for you and do that. But do get out there and orchestrate bringing new people into your life in your own way. It is worth the risk!

– ACTIVITY –
ARE YOU A PARTY ANIMAL?

There are several different types of social gatherings. Even if you aren't comfortable at one type, you may very well be the life of the party at another.

Think about the kinds of gatherings you like and dislike and why. In your notebook, on a fresh page, list the types of social events that you are most likely to attend across the top. For example, you might be expected to attend weddings, friends' parties, company functions, networking events, or family gatherings. Draw lines in between each of these to create columns.

In each column, brainstorm how each function makes you feel and list adjectives about each. For example:

Weddings	Friend's Party	Networking Event
Family	Noise	Large room
Strangers	Drinking	Crowds
Dancing	Strangers	Strangers
Noise	Awkward	Performance
Obligation	Crowded	Draining
Stuffy	Exciting	Anxiety

Are you the type of person who is more comfortable at loud, exciting events or in quiet, more structured events? Do you like to be around a handful of people or surrounded by them? When do you feel most comfortable and yourself? Do crowds of people make it hard for you to concentrate or hear?

Are there common themes in each type of event? Circle any repeated feelings and adjectives, and think about ways to overcome these hurdles. Perhaps being uncomfortable with not knowing anyone there is a reason you don't care for an event. Could you bring someone with you to these events so that you are never alone while you interact with someone new? If you are often drained during events, can you make it a habit to rest afterward and take time during to recharge? You can make an unfavorable event work better for you if you move away from the crowd, go with a friend, or look for another introvert in the crowd with whom you can commiserate. Having a strategy before you face the situation will definitely make it more productive.

Chapter 2
Building Blocks of Success

Perhaps you chose to be invisible. Maybe it happened over time. However you came to a place where you feel like you blend in, it is time to step from the shadows and become the kind of person who has undeniable charisma. When you become a compelling force in your job, you also open up opportunities for success and advancement in your larger community, which makes you a known expert and resource. Not only will you be valued among your network of friends and associates, but also your appeal will draw others to you, creating prospects for more and stronger relationships. Your greater success and happiness ultimately depend on your magnetism and the excitement that you can generate about yourself. Just because you are an introvert does not mean that you are not or cannot be charismatic.

There are basic building blocks of business success: yourself, your business intelligence, your ability to connect, and your network. By strengthening each of these aspects of your life, you will emerge from the shadows as someone who attracts positive attention, is a leader, and who makes great things happen.

BUILDING BLOCKS OF BUSINESS SUCCESS

1. Self. Focus on improving your confidence, overcoming your fears, and recognizing your limitations. As you work on ways to improve yourself—and this includes how you present yourself to other people—you will also need to recognize things that restrict you. You have a set number of hours in your day, and that means delegating some of the responsibilities that you cannot do in that time. Choose the highest-value activities to do yourself, and find ways to off-load your daily to-dos that are your "time sinks."

2. Business Acumen. Acknowledge that you desire promotion, leadership, or other positive opportunities. Your career is an area that truly has near-limitless possibilities. You can do and be just about anything you want. If you desire the employee-of-the-month award, a promotion, or an entire career change, this is the time to make it happen.

3. Connection. Learn how to establish better connections with others, including friends, coworkers, and business associates. Introverts often struggle with making easy connections with people. Fearing awkwardness, many introverts shy away from establishing and growing relationships. Simple steps can be taken to ensure comfort for you and for the people you meet. Relax, enjoy, and learn from each new encounter.

4. Network. Grow and nurture your business network to build your business opportunities and support your overall goals. Your network is your secret weapon and the way that you will be able to knock down doors and keep a steady prospect list, thus providing yourself with advancement opportunities.

I will occasionally run into someone I went to high school with in a business setting, at a meeting, or at an event. It is always interesting to see how I am received now, because I was so unexceptional as a student. In many situations, I am leading the meeting or giving the presentation, and somehow this must alter the memory of my former classmates. In my own recollection of high school, I was an outsider. I was lonely, quiet, and admittedly a little odd. I felt I did not fit in and tried only halfheartedly. But to hear my classmates now try to place me in their own memories, you would think I had actually been a pretty popular student. "Weren't you a cheerleader?" they ask. Or, "You had the lead in that play, didn't you?" Even, "Do you still talk to anyone from the team?" These questions always make me smile. No, of course I wasn't a cheerleader or the lead in the play or on any team, ever. I was the quiet girl who ate lunch in the media room and did homework alone in the back of the dark auditorium during study hall. But no one remembers this because I was invisible back then. They assume I must have been in the middle of all the school activities because today I just seem like that kind of person. Today I work to force myself out of my comfort zone, and I understand the need to make myself heard and to walk with the confidence an introvert can gain only with hard work and experience.

Out from the darkness, into the spotlight. (Of course, I mean in the spotlight only occasionally, and on my own terms, when the situation dictates, and as long as I get a nap afterward—but no one else needs to know that!)

SELF-BELIEF

Believing in yourself and in your power to succeed is sometimes particularly difficult for introverts. Because we generally do not seek positive feedback or even constructive criticism from others, we are often not given any. We put our heads down and do our work, and we are left alone because eventually people think or understand that this is what we want.

As you go about your life, it is easy to be caught up in the expectations of others, the pull on you from all of the outside influences of work, family, and society. It is not always a bad thing for you to be challenged by life and to struggle; however, as you go through these times, you have to be careful not to lose yourself in the process.

As a student I was taught not to label people. I assume that the intention of this well-meaning advice was to teach us to treat others nicely and not to discriminate on the basis of a characteristic or set of characteristics (all of you nerds, geeks, cool kids, posers, and jocks out there know what I am talking about).

But labels are generally just adjectives used to describe people—sometimes several adjectives are used at the same time, and for good reason. "Introvert" is one of them, but there are a few adjectives that I use to describe myself in addition to introvert. I am any and all of these words at any given time, and how I perceive myself can be very empowering. You too should be able to gain strength from knowing that you have the ability to be so many wonderful things. And you can look to the traits that you wish you could include in your list and work to add these to your inventory. Your self-perception and understanding of self are some of the most important factors in your success.

Believe in and know yourself and your ability to achieve greatness, and you will achieve that greatness.

– ACTIVITY –
HOW WOULD YOU DESCRIBE YOURSELF?

Take your notebook and on the left side of a fresh sheet write "I am." Then list the adjectives that describe you now. On the right side write "I will be," and list the adjectives that describe who you want to be. I've provided an example below if you need some ideas to get you started. Your answers should reveal some of your hidden energy. Can you gain strength from these descriptors? Be aware of how some words may seem negative but can have an alternate positive meaning. The purpose of this activity is to get you to recognize your positive qualities and give you traits that you can work toward. Go ahead—label yourself!

I am...	I will be...	
Shy	Confident	Charming
Forceful	Educated	Driven
Beautiful	Likable	Focused
Timid	Fun	Ingenious
Powerful	Bold	Strong
Intelligent	Empathetic	Aggressive
Thoughtful	Caring	Artistic
Industrious	Organized	Trusting
Complex	Quiet	Stubborn
Curious	Irresistible	Animated
Courageous	Positive	
Persistent	Brave	
Brazen	Innovative	
Cautious	Secure	
Introverted	Adventurous	
Wise	Creative	
Predictable	Inspiring	

BUSINESS ACUMEN

Being great in most businesses has to be a true passion in order for the introvert to achieve success. This is because most companies require their managers and leadership teams to be strong, charismatic, and respected. They expect comfortable social interaction and speaking skills. Many introverts are satisfied with just being mediocre in business because they are fearful or uncomfortable with the risk of exposing themselves. They may be able to accept success in other areas of their lives, as good parents, in sports, or at home. It is common for introverts not to be interested in drawing attention to themselves or learning how to better handle their introversion in order to break down the barriers to career advancement. As I've said before, success is self-determined, but business mediocrity is not for me, and if you're reading this book, you've probably decided that it's not for you either. And that means that to be great in business, you will have to increase your business intelligence.

As a young, introverted salesperson, I found it difficult at times to pick up the telephone to speak with someone to schedule a meeting. Now cold-calling is something that many salespeople struggle with, but much of the time, especially early in my career, I was calling on prospects that had already been introduced to me. I am the kind of person who doesn't like to order a pizza, so calling someone to set up a meeting so that I could sell them something was daunting.

Sitting in my office and staring at the phone day after day gave me plenty of time to find ways to get around this vital aspect of sales—some good and some bad. Ultimately, the thing that saved me was a good habit that my mom had instilled in me—card writing. In a day when cell phone calls can be made and email can be sent from nearly anywhere, at any time, a card is a pleasant and tactile gift to a recipient.

Perhaps as a way to procrastinate picking up the phone (or maybe because I had a great business instinct), I began to write cards after meeting anyone new. I would take their business card, and nearly immediately after getting back to my office, I would write a nice little note, include my own business card, even if they already had one, and tell them that I looked forward to our future conversations.

It was simple, but it solidified a connection. By writing a note, I had opened the door to call to see whether they had received the card, and I gave them the information and opening needed for them to make that step to call or email themselves. Even better, most people were grateful to have such a nicety extended to them. It was a tool that I used to feel more comfortable, but it was also one that gave me something special and memorable. I stood apart. My sales increased after that because I found a way to manage my introversion and overcome my fear, but not in a way that betrayed who I am.

I value the work that I do too highly to settle for anything less than perfection. But I realized that some situations are better for learning. Do I understand that I will rarely be perfect? Of course I do. But I would rather have room for improvement in work than believe that less than my best is acceptable.

Driven by a desire to succeed, a thirst for knowledge, and the need to be greater than you were before, you will find your own ways to manage your introversion. You will find that it is more important for you to do well in your career than it is to feel comfortable all the time—especially if you know that, after a long day of work, you can retreat to your quiet place and recharge.

CREATING CONNECTION

To be able to effectively network, the introvert must be able to find a connection that binds two people together, such as common interests, age, background, or experience. With nearly everyone you meet, you should be able to find something about that person on which your connection can begin.

A couple of months ago, I met with a gentleman from my networking group, which I had recently joined. The man was an HR administrator at a manufacturing company. He was in his early fifties, grew up in the South, and was African American. He was unmarried, had no children, and was very religious.

Going into this meeting I thought to myself, *What will I have in common with this man? We are two very different people, with very different backgrounds. Our jobs are not similar, nor are our personal or family situations.*

As I sat down with this gentleman, I was struck by his strong voice and friendly eyes. He was a man that exuded confidence and experience, and soon our conversation turned to new media. He had a passion for the Internet and how marketing has changed as more companies begin to fully embrace online social networking.

And there it was. This was a topic that I too was passionate about, and the next thirty minutes were filled with excited banter about all that can be done with new technologies, how the market will change over the next decade, ways businesses can use the emerging technologies, and the downfalls to different applications. He and I made a connection, and we have had a wonderful networking relationship since.

Despite my trepidation, I walked into the meeting knowing that to be successful in making a connection, I would have to find a commonality. It took several questions and time to find it, but once we were able to establish that, the rest of the conversation went smoothly on all topics and we built rapport.

We don't always get to choose the people that enter our lives, but if we make an effort to find the commonality, we can begin to form a strong relationship—to build our network and increase our opportunities for success.

NETWORK KNOWLEDGE

Your network is your support system. It will guide you, teach you, push you, and ask for the same in return. As you learn about how your network of friends and business associates interweaves with your life and success, you will be taken to a higher level of understanding of yourself, your career, how others see you, and your role in the business world. I cannot stress more the importance of knowing your network.

There is a theory that there are six degrees of separation between you and every other person on the planet—and with the technology available today, it is even easier to make these connections. That means that your network literally extends around the world. You have a connection through the people you know to anyone you wish to know. This is a huge asset to the introvert, who may not be aggressive in extending his or her own circle of influence. Everyone knows someone, and the people you know may have contacts that will be beneficial to you and to whom you may also be a great asset, friend, vendor, or connection.

Beyond the traditional ways of building your network, such as networking events and meeting people through personal introduction, new technologies make networking even more accessible for introverts. Online social media such as Internet forums, blogs, Twitter, Facebook, MySpace, and LinkedIn (and the new sites that appear daily) are a popular and comfortable way to begin networking and to continue growing long-lasting, mutually beneficial business relationships. I am a strong advocate of using these applications to establish connections and maintain them, but I also believe that old-fashioned one-to-one in-person networking is ideal. If you use these new ways to network, use them as supplements, not as the only way you relate to others. These new websites and applications do not exist as a crutch for introverts but rather as a tool. Much can be lost in a text message, and much can be gained in a facial expression. So know your network—and know the limitation of your networking tools.

– ACTIVITY –
YOUR CIRCLE OF INFLUENCE

On a fresh sheet in your notebook, draw a circle in the middle and write your name in it.

1. Draw ten circles around yours and fill in the names of the ten people you are closest to, such as your family, best friends, spouse, and so on.

2. Next, draw ten more circles on the page and fill those with ten more people with whom you have a relationship of some kind. Include your coworkers, friends, and neighbors.

3. Next, connect lines out from your circle in the center to the people in your life, and draw lines among the circles if those people have a connection.

Your drawing will first look like the spokes of a wheel and may even begin to look like a web. Do you see the different ways that the people in your life form a network around you? Are there areas on your chart that do not have many connections? Take this further by adding other people in your life to the chart, keeping an eye on ways that you can make more connections.

If you have many great connections with people you consider friends but fewer connections with people you know from work, then consider ways to expand your network in this area. If you have great family relationships, look at ways to meet more of the people whom they know. Remember that we are all connected, and as an introvert a personal introduction from a friend or family member will go a long way toward increasing your comfort level and success.

Chapter 3
First Steps

Whenever life challenges us we discover a little more about ourselves. Struggle often begets clarity of purpose and a renewed sense of self. Being an introvert who wants to be noticed can be a huge challenge—and so in having this purpose, you will learn and grow and gain confidence in that pursuit.

You may have a decent idea of who you are or you may be one of those many folks who feel the need to go find themselves. My suggestion is always to take the time to seriously ponder the contribution you would like to make to the world, the legacy you wish to leave, and the things you would like to accomplish. But to reach a certain level of professional success, you need to take the first step of knowing not only who you are but also where you are headed. It is safe to assume that if you have made it this far into the book, you recognize something in yourself that you would like to improve. Your goal may be a grand plan or it may be a simpler goal like becoming a better public speaker. Knowing and accepting where you are in life and the person who you are, regardless of your flaws or challenges, is important for reaching the goals that you set. These things will no doubt change as age and experience open up facets of your life and future of which you were not yet aware. However, don't be afraid to accept that over time these things may change.

When I left for college I knew who I was. I was the best young theatrical technician Ithaca College had ever seen. That was until I arrived there and realized that there were a dozen other young theatrical technicians and that most of them had more experience, success, and expertise than I did. And they each thought they were the best too (this would be the "big fish, small pond" thing my parents had warned me about).

After college I worked in several jobs. Despite working consistently through college at professional theaters, after graduation I never worked as a theater tech again. It was no longer who I was. I had to reevaluate my interests, my other responsibilities, and my skills several times as I moved through my career. My résumé is evidence of my varied background and multiple changes of direction. Your success may require several steps, or it may necessitate a complete change of direction as mine has (many, many times).

Who are you now? And where are you going?

REALISTIC GOALS

To succeed, you need to understand why you aren't currently as successful as you want to be. It is important to evaluate how realistic your goals are. There are, of course, factors that you can't control in your life. Take your height, for example. Several studies have shown that tall people earn more money over a lifetime. There isn't too much you can do about that besides work even harder, be smarter, and perhaps wear good shoes with a little extra lift or heal. And of course, as my father always said, "Stand up straight and proud."

There aren't many factors that you can't change that will keep you from success. However, your definition of success and the goals that will get you there may need to be reevaluated. I will most likely (being a thirty-three-year-old, 5' 5" woman) never make it as a professional basketball player. It is not impossible, just very unlikely. To have a goal of success that is defined by unreasonable expectations is not only setting up a failure scenario; it is irresponsible.

Your success may be defined by having a rewarding career and enough time and money to take a vacation once a year. It may be defined by being vice president of your company, having a home-based business, or winning that community service award. It may be defined by all of those things. The key is to be realistic, optimistic, and focused. The more determined you are, the greater the likelihood that you will meet those goals and be a success—but the question of possibility must be asked. Also, remember that there are people out there who want to help you. Don't be afraid to ask or seek out advice from your trusted network of friends and family.

GETTING OUT AND BEING ON

A pivotal moment in my life as an acknowledged introvert came several years ago when I attended an open networking event. I had been receiving email information about this regularly occurring event for months, but I had always found a reason not to attend, until one dreadful day. My supervisor came into my office and asked whether I had ever made it to the popular event.

Ugh! I thought to myself. I told my boss that I hadn't had a chance, and then he, of course, requested that I go to see whether I could make some new contacts. We needed to meet new people and grow the business, and there "would be good prospects there," he said. *OK*, I thought to myself, *how bad could it be?* With that little kick, I had the motivation, and I agreed that I would go that night. So I stuffed my pockets full of business cards and set out. I was determined to go out there, make some new contacts, and make my boss proud!

I practiced my elevator speech and had pretend conversations with myself the entire drive over. When I arrived that evening, I dutifully got my name tag, grabbed a drink, and found my favorite event corner (you know the one: it's in the back, away from the crowd, near something interesting to look at). I proceeded to stand in that corner and then transition to another corner, carefully examine the artwork, get another drink, read a brochure that had been left on a table, and then I left. I was there for about an hour and did not meet anyone—not one single person. I didn't even try to make eye contact—in fact, I avoided it at all costs. I left in complete despair, frustrated with myself and disappointed that I had both wasted my time and not had the guts to talk with anyone and hand out a few business cards. Even worse, I would have to explain to my boss why I didn't do my job.

I swore that I would never again attend another business networking event and not do any networking. My own challenging networking scenario had played out over and over again throughout my career. I knew that I needed to network, but those kinds of networking events just did not work for me. I recognized the value in creating a group of valued friends, advisers, and business associates, but I was unable to build my network much beyond my immediate family and a few close friends (most of whom I would never have considered actually asking a business-related question).

I tried several other avenues for business networking, including joining professional organizations and volunteer groups. My hope was that these more structured groups would afford me the opportunities and comfort I was seeking. I found that while there were plenty of events and lunches to attend, I still shied away from networking and meeting new people.

Then, the first of two epiphanies happened. I had finally had enough of boring lunches that I attended just to leave without a single new contact and of awkward after-work events that never seemed conducive to building business relationships. So I began looking at opportunities to meet with people one-on-one.

At first I was apprehensive about doing this, yet I was so frustrated with the way things

> ### shy girl tip:
> *One-on-One Meetings*
>
> As a person who flourishes in situations where you can completely focus on the task at hand, take the opportunity to meet with people one-on-one for a better connection.

had gone that it seemed the only sensible next step. I was very excited—and relieved—to find that my invitations were warmly received and readily accepted. These meetings proved very beneficial and rewarding, and I made it part of my regular routine to meet with new people for lunch or coffee. As an introvert, the more personal, quiet setting allowed me to really get to know these people, and them, me. In addition, I stopped feeling guilty about missing the lunches and happy hours. My contact list was growing, and my relationships grew stronger.

My second epiphany happened after a friend of mine suggested that I go to a formal networking meeting called Business Network International (BNI). I went alone to my first early-morning BNI breakfast meeting and was immediately greeted at the door. A friendly woman helped me sign in, gave me a name tag, and gave me a quick overview of the agenda. She then helped me get a bagel and some tea and then went around to each person in the room and introduced me as if we had been friends for years. We sat down at a table and she explained parts of the meeting as they happened. I was impressed by the formulaic approach of BNI and the way each member knew why he or she was there and how everyone supported one another's businesses. I immediately felt included, and all of my fears about being an outsider were extinguished. This setup worked well for me because the group met regularly, so I got to know everyone in a short span of time. Everyone knew what was expected of them, from attendance to participation. I have been attending BNI meetings ever since.

This particular group setting is a lot less intimidating for the introvert. The regular agenda of BNI takes the guesswork out of when you will be speaking and about what. They happily accept new members in cities across the United States and internationally, and you will find that this group, and others like it, cater to people who need that structure and are serious about building their networks. While you will find introverts and extroverts in these organizations, it is a very comfortable environment, especially if you are apprehensive about meeting new people or about public speaking.

These two steps alleviated my own desperation and frustration over networking. I began to rebuild my self-confidence, and my network began to grow. Subsequently, my business also began to grow.

I cannot stress enough the importance of business networking. It brings people together and makes businesses succeed. You may be reading this because you are a salesperson or have been put in the role of a salesperson. You may work for a small company that needs every employee to represent it and bring in new business to succeed. Or you may be a business owner or sole proprietor who must take on a variety of roles, including sales. No matter how you come to know that there is always the need for and value in business networking, I guarantee that you will get out of it what you put in—and often more.

Whatever your motivation for improving your network and overcoming the hurdles of being shy, your ability to recognize that you are strong enough to put yourself out there and take a chance ultimately determines your success. You may be the only one who will ever know that you are shy or uncomfortable, and you need to know that you may fit better in some places than others. Moreover, there is strength that can be gained from being a little uncomfortable and then getting through the situation. Take a chance, stand up, and give that presentation; say "hello" to a stranger; go to an event you are uncomfortable at; or find a group in which you can feel comfortable. Eventually it does get easier, and you may even start to think that it's fun.

– ACTIVITY –
MAKE NETWORKING EASIER

Do you find networking events intimidating? Before your next networking event or opportunity to network, take out your pad of paper and consider how the event could play out. Write down the questions you have and then your answers. For example:

Question: "What will I do first thing as I get through the door?"
Think about this scenario and take yourself there in your mind. Feel the emotions, see the room, hear the noises, and then picture taking action. Let your answer come to you.

Possible Answer: "If I don't see someone I know, I will find a good place to work from—a side of the room or the quieter corner. Then I will look for someone standing alone and approach that person, introduce myself, and ask about him or her."

Listening to your inner voice is a strategy for working through an introvert's fears and trepidation about these kinds of situations. The act of putting these questions on paper takes away their power over you as your answers empower you. The more you practice your own mindfulness, the easier it will become.

BEING A FORCED EXTROVERT

There were several steps in my progression to being what my friend Paul calls a forced extrovert. It is, by admission, a silly idea, but it was an important realization for me. Most people wouldn't consider me much of an introvert at all these days, but I assure you that I still am and that every day I am forced by circumstance to be a little more out there than my comfort zone would prefer.

As I have said before, I also have a touch of stage fright (OK, "touch" doesn't even begin to describe the sheer panic that paralyzes me when asked to give a speech). This stage fright manifests itself at the most inopportune times, when looking like an idiot is less than preferable for a favorable impression. There are so many examples of my stage fright getting the best of me as a student that I could probably fill an entire book with those sad stories—but that would make for a rather pathetic book. The point is that stage fright has been a problem for me as long as I can remember, and it was one that haunted me into adulthood.

A few years ago I was taking an adult-education class after work. We had been told that we were going to have to give a short presentation in front of a small group. I was stressed out and nervous, but I had prepared for my speech, I had practiced, I had copied all my handouts, and I was pretty sure that I was ready. It took almost all my courage to go to that class knowing that I would have to give that presentation, but I convinced myself that I could give a decent, casual ten-minute speech to a handful of people. I had done it before, and I knew my material. I just had to relax and do it.

So I took a deep breath—and walked in.

When I sat down, the instructor casually informed us that we would not be breaking into small groups as previously announced but rather would be giving the presentation to the entire class. This was a large group of scary strangers who had no reason to like me or pretend that what I was saying made any sense at all (unlike my employees). As I sat in horror, trying to collect myself, a video camera was wheeled out from the corner of the room and pointed at the podium.

I was mortified and I was mad—very mad. I had to escape. I pushed back from the table, stood up from my seat, and as the news began to sink in, I raced—as nonchalantly as possible—into the bathroom.

I stood in that tiny, dark, dirty bathroom stall, and I sobbed. I cried uncontrollably because I felt betrayed by the instructor who had misled me and changed the format of the presentation. But I was primarily upset because I was upset. Why was this little presentation to a classroom of people so difficult for me to give? I was an adult. I was a professional, I had given speeches and led meetings before; I had given literally dozens of presentations, and I was prepared to give this one, but the rules had changed, and I was not in charge.

Instead of five people I sort of knew, there were thirty people I mostly did not know. To add to my anguish, the presentation was going to be videotaped, and that added a dimension that for some reason shook me to my core.

The difference between this and the other presentations was that I had learned over the years to control my environment. I gave speeches and presentations on my own terms. If I had to drag out my public-speaking self, I filled the room with allies, adjusted the lighting, and had the podium or microphone at the right height, rehearsed until I knew the speech by heart, and still, more often than not, I read from my notes. And it was never, ever videotaped.

> ### shy girl tip:
> #### Public Speaking
>
> Not only practice what you will say but also go into the space in which you will be speaking. Know where you will stand, how the tables or chairs are set, and what technical challenges there may be. Knowing the space in which you are to speak will take the anxiety out of walking into an unfamiliar place.

As I stood there in that bathroom, upset and feeling humiliated, and yet without cause, I realized that no one was going to come in there and rescue me. No matter what I did, if I wanted to avoid total embarrassment, I would have to collect myself and give my presentation, for better or for worse—and so I did.

My presentation was probably less than stellar. I spoke too fast, stuttered over my words, and paced at the front of the room—but I got through it. That instructor I was so mad at, as far as I know, never even knew I had been upset.

She and the other instructors thanked me and told me the presentation went well. I figured if they couldn't recognize or weren't concerned with the fact that I was shaking uncontrollably and was so nervous I stuttered, babbled, and paced (and that I had run to the bathroom and cried my eyes out moments before), perhaps I was making a bigger deal out of it than the situation merited. I did it, good or bad, and I needed to move on.

You and I both know people for whom this situation will never make sense. They don't know how terrifying public speaking can be, or why sometimes it is fine and others not. These people will never understand the horror and anxiety that public speaking causes—yet it remains the number-one fear of people everywhere. So we are not alone! Looking back, it is embarrassing to retell my story, but I learned something important and worth sharing that day: be prepared, practice, and accept that you may not always have control. Public speaking can be an intimidating prospect, but it is one that is necessary for leadership, and it is one that you can practice and improve on. The introvert controls by nature, by isolating him- or herself but remaining silent, by making thoughtful choices, but it is not always possible to do these things. By learning to make the best of the situation, handle change, and be as prepared as possible, you too can improve your speaking skills.

I still don't like giving presentations, but I realized that I could do it even when the rules changed, when I did not control every factor, when I was outside of my comfort zone, or even when I was being videotaped (although the thought of this still makes my heart race). As time went on, the more speaking I did, the more confident I became and the better the presentations went. Sometimes I just had to go with it, jump in. Admittedly, I will never be comfortable up on stage or in front of a class or in a big meeting, but it does get just a little better each time.

– ACTIVITY –
MAKE PUBLIC SPEAKING EASIER

What makes public speaking scary for you? Is it fear of rejection or of not being perfect? Are you afraid you will forget what you are supposed to say or that people won't understand what you are trying to say? How can you change these factors to make public speaking easier for you? Will preparation, practice, and notes make you a better speaker? Are there aspects of the presentation that you can control?

Write the words "Dislike," "Why," and "Action" on a fresh sheet of paper in your notepad. First, we must identify what it is that makes public speaking such a challenge. Second, we must ask why. Third, we can identify an action to take. For example:

Dislike	Why	Action
Feeling in my stomach	I feel sick	Drink water, breathe
My hands shake	Shows nervousness	Hold podium
Value/importance others place	I might let them down	Give my best
How I will look	I might look silly/stupid	Practice speech

Identify why you are uncomfortable speaking in public and find opportunities to practice your style, find the best delivery, ease your comfort level, and improve your performance.

REACHING EQUILIBRIUM (REALIGNING, PRIORITIZING, BALANCING)

Before making any abrupt and enormous changes in your life or the way you go about meeting people, doing your job, or joining organizations, you also need to look at all of your other obligations.

You need to take into account your family, spouse, children (and their ages), classes that you are taking, and other responsibilities. It will do you no good at all to forfeit sleep for weeks on end to succeed in your business or job (trust me, I have tried). Ultimately, if you don't take all factors into consideration, you will most likely sabotage your chances of long-term success.

After the birth of my son, I found myself in a flustered and chaotic state. I figured a new mom was supposed to be flustered and chaotic, and so I tried to embrace the mayhem and do it all myself at least for the first few months. And then—well, the sleepless nights, the nursing of the baby while doing business conference calls from my living room, and the pressure of being everything to everyone started to get to me.

And it was obvious to everyone but me.

My son's pediatrician sensed that the weight of the world was on me during a routine visit. She casually asked if I was working—to which I just smirked. The idea that a new mother was doing anything but working was ridiculous, but I let it go and just said, "Yes." Then quickly, as if rehearsed, pushed by some force or guilt or sense of women's lib, I added that I was so lucky because I could work from home, that I had a home office and a terrific boss and a super job. Life was perfect! She smiled the way a woman does when she knows, and then said in what I perceived at the time to be rather cold, "Sometimes working from home is the worst thing to do for the baby and for you."

I bristled.

She then touched my hand and said something prophetic that I will never forget, and I hope you will take with you as well. She said in a soft, motherly voice, "You can have it all. You just can't have it all at the same time."

I left the doctor's office feeling as if I had been kicked in the gut. Why couldn't I have it all? Wasn't I the new generation of empowered, strong women that had the world wrapped around our little pinky fingers? Who was she to tell me what I could have and when I could have it?

And then it sunk in—sleep is nice. Time with the baby is better when not negotiating business deals, and work is best done when it can be the focus of the time spent doing it. Nursing and conference calls don't mix (although technically possible). And most of all, my husband deserves a wife who doesn't stay up working until two o'clock every morning. In short, she was right. I couldn't have it all, not at the same time, at least not without help.

It is with that cautionary tale that I tell you to remember that each aspect of your life affects every other thing.

Introverts internalize. They forget to delegate, and they don't ask for help. As you take on additional tasks and goals, it will mean that you will have to learn to let go of control over everything if you ever expect to be great at anything. Keep your highest priorities in mind at all times and realign your priorities if necessary. Ask for help, and seek out opportunities to let others into your life. It may become obvious, as it did for me: for every thing there is a season, which, at that moment, meant cutting my work hours back, getting more help with my son, and being disciplined about not working when the baby was awake and my husband was home.

Taking the business world by storm could wait, at least for a while.

OUTSOURCING THE SMALL STUFF

By the time my son was about nineteen months old, I was back to working full-time again (or "full-time plus," since I worked early mornings, late nights, and weekends to accommodate my family). It was a full schedule, but I thought I had plenty of help. My son was at a sitter two full days a week, my mom watched him two half days, my husband stayed home a half a day, and I had another sitter come to the house at least a few hours each week. This carefully orchestrated weekly routine seemed to work for us, and I figured that if I had child care covered, I was doing OK. However, it became obvious (again) that I still could not do it all. My priorities were time with my family and doing well in my job, but I had not taken into account some of the basics, and as a result, I wasn't meeting either of my two main priorities well.

I had to take a look at all the things that were my time sinks—everything that I did that did not have positive return on my time investment. On that list was everything from deleting spam email to sorting bills, writing proposals and business correspondence, and picking out my outfits for work in the morning. It was overwhelming to look at the list of things I did on a regular basis and how much time was lost to the seemingly mundane but somehow important.

Then I did it—I hired someone to buy my groceries!

It sounds ridiculous, I know, especially because I lived in the suburbs and the grocery store was only a couple of miles away. Not to mention that I am not the kind of person who normally asks for help or admits that I can't accomplish one of the most basic of human chores. However, when I looked at how I spent my weeks, I was investing a lot of time either grocery shopping or running to the store to buy one or two things to get me through the next few days. For about $20 plus the cost of the groceries every other week, I bought back two hours of my life! Well worth the investment.

I realized that I had reverted to a very introverted tendency of not looking for ways I could take the assistance of other people. When I was able to come to terms with this, I began to look at my other time sinks and was able to outsource some of them as well. I hired a company to come and help me organize my closets to help me cut down on the time I spend choosing clothes in the morning (they were a mess: clothes on the floor, winter clothes mixed in with summer clothes, maternity clothes mixed with my new "skinny" clothes). I hired an assistant at work to take care of my calendar, scheduling, organizing, and correspondence. I looked at everything I did and didn't dismiss an opportunity to outsource any chore or responsibility until I measured the cost of outsourcing and the time I could gain back by doing so.

And suddenly, my business started booming.

Realizing that I couldn't do it all but that I still had options available to get it done was a huge relief. I had been afraid to ask for help and delegate when possible to achieve the goals I had set for myself, but if I looked at my life as a business, and my business as a business (and not just a time-sucking, life-draining job), I could get more done. I could work with a team to accomplish the tasks that required completion, reprioritize the things that could wait, and turn my personal attention to the big-picture items that would most benefit from my own input. And I could still spend quality time with my family; in fact, I could spend more time with my family. To accomplish what I wanted to achieve for myself as a professional, I needed to become very efficient, and that meant that just because I could do something didn't mean that I should. If my time could be better spent working on my business, or with my family, or doing those other things that were important in my life, there was a greater value in that. The value of my time was worth more than what it cost to get that time back.

If you look at most successful professionals, you will find that they too came to the same realization: outsourcing is often mission critical to success. There are only twenty-four hours in a day. We all get the same twenty-four hours. How you chose to spend them is your decision and your responsibility.

– ACTIVITY –
LOG YOUR TIME

Log your time each day for one week. From the time you wake up until you go to sleep at night, record how much time you spend doing each activity. Here are some examples:

- Getting ready for work
- Tending to family needs (e.g., getting your children ready, grocery shopping)
- Personal care
- Working
- At work but not working
- Checking personal email
- Personal finances
- Commuting
- Housework
- Fun and recreation

At the end of the week, examine the results. Are you spending considerable time doing low-value activities? Are you not spending time on the things that you deem important? What can you outsource to free up time for your priorities?

Chapter 4

What Is Your Business IQ?

One of the most important aspects of success (and overall happiness) is doing what you love to do. However, if you love your job and are good at it, you are only partway to success—you must be recognized for your hard work and accomplishments. These factors and your ability to affect them constitute your Business IQ.

shy girl tip:
Loving Your Job

When you wake up in the morning are you excited to go to work? If you can't answer yes to this question at least three days a week, you should consider a change.

I hope you love your job. If not, set this book down immediately and take a good, hard look at your career choice. It is impossible to be a true success in your career unless you are dedicated, and you can't be dedicated unless you love your job. (Then remember to pick this book up again when you figure it out!) Dedication takes too much work to be directed at a job that you do not love.

Being good at what you do and being recognized for it is the key. Learn the rules, understand the expectations, and work to achieve your goals. Recognition comes when you do well at what you do and others know it. However, as an introvert, recognition may have made you uncomfortable in the past, and others, seeing your discomfort, may not be giving you what you deserve just to save you from that discomfort! You are going to have to learn not only to embrace recognition but also to seek it out.

Yes, I said, "Seek it out!"

Ask for recognition. Don't get me wrong—don't go buy a T-shirt that says, "Hello I'm good at my job and I deserve recognition," but you may have to have a heart-to-heart with a supervisor and point out areas where you have achieved, exceeded goals, and risen to the top. You may have to send or have your human resources department send out notice to the media of an award you receive, or of a promotion, or of a new product that you are launching. Don't expect that if you do your job well people will always notice and shower you with praise. Unfortunately, the world doesn't usually work that way.

Putting these elements together, you will begin to build your own Business IQ and head further down that path to success.

FOURTEEN WAYS TO SELF-PROMOTE

OK, here it is—the big secret. If you wait around it may not happen, and you will fall farther behind those who know. What am I talking about? Self-promotion.

I'm sorry I had to break it to you. If you are invisible to the world, it doesn't matter how good you are. So get noticed. How does an introvert get that recognition? The answer is: steps. Take small steps in your quest for promotion, first taking on the things that are easiest for you, and then taking on the more challenging.

Here are some ways to self-promote and be more visible.

1. Create an email signature. In your email program, you can create a signature that appears each time you start a new message. Include your name, title, and contact information but also something like, "Ask me about our half-price guarantee!" or "Winner of the 2008 Gold Circle Award."

2. Change your voice mail daily. Few people change their message each day, but this is a great way to tell the people who call you that you have attention to detail and an interest in staying current. Include a quote of the day or a message about the day: "It may be rainy today in Brighton, New York, but your call will brighten my day! Thanks for calling."

3. Get a website or blog. Create a place where you can write about subjects that interest you and that relate to your business. Begin to establish yourself as an expert in your field. The online community doesn't care whether you are shy as long as you can write and you have unique ideas or an interesting way of expressing yourself.

4. Find a local business publication that works with freelance writers and write articles for it. There is a good chance you won't get paid, but you can use these articles to promote yourself and your business and potentially get paid for your writing later on. Use these articles when meeting with prospects or to strengthen your relationship with your customers. While on maternity leave, I began reading a lot of business journals and technology websites to stay current. After I went back to work, I kept up my reading and noticed that several of them were seeking submissions. In one case, I met with the local editor, and we brainstormed several areas on which I could write. My articles were posted on the Web and in the print version with my picture, my bio, and my company information. This was an excellent way for me to generate some additional interest in my company and in me after being out of the loop for several months.

5. Get to know the media. Make an effort to know at least a couple members of your local media. Newspaper reporters, television news anchors, news directors, editors, and radio personalities are all looking for great subjects to report on. By bringing these people into your network, you will become a valued and important resource to them. Give them a good story, and they will come back to you again and again.

6. Find a public relations buddy. Do you know another deserving but underrecognized individual who you can trust with a little covert operation? Share your hopes and ambitions with this person, tell him or her about accolades you would like to receive, and offer to nominate your friend for an award or write a public-interest story about them. Ask them to do the same for you.

7. Send out a monthly or quarterly personal e-newsletter. An associate of mine sends out an email newsletter monthly to everyone in his distribution list. His is similar to a Christmas letter ("We just moved into out new office," "We have a new product at work," "The weather has been great"), and over the years, I feel that I have gotten to know him better from this monthly letter. Just remember that you are sending this out to your business associates, so there is no need to get too personal! Most people won't care that your niece has chicken pox and that you just bought new lawn furniture, so keep it mostly business.

8. Have a professional bio written. Hire a professional résumé and biography writer. The bio can be used on your website, when applying for executive positions, or when nominated for awards. A decent bio written by someone else can tout your accomplishments in ways you might feel uncomfortable doing yourself! This same person can also write an incredible résumé for you for the same reason.

9. Offer to speak at seminars or schedule your own.
Speaking at seminars is a wonderful way to promote yourself and your business. If the big seminar-style opportunity
doesn't feel comfortable for you, look for roundtables or
panel discussions at which you can speak. They are more
casual, and there will be more than one speaker, so you won't
have to be all alone on stage or at the front of the room. A
few years ago, I was asked to participate at a Women in
Computers discussion on networking and mentorship at a
local university. I hadn't ever taken part in a panel discussion before and didn't know what to expect. But it was a lot
of fun, and since then I have become a big fan of this type
of setting for networking, education, and self-promotion. I
found that it was good to have other speakers there to fill
in the gaps when I needed a little help answering a question, and I learned a lot from the variety of participants. The
environment was relaxed, and I was relatively comfortable,
came across well, and had a lot to add to the discussion.
No matter the forum, take the opportunity to get yourself
noticed by your community and industry.

10. Make time. Schedule regular meetings with your supervisor, CEO, or mentor in your company. While it may be
impossible to meet each time, setting a meeting on the
calendar will keep you top of mind, and when you do get the
chance to sit down, you will have the opportunity to discuss
your progress on your current projects. Face time with the
boss is important, so do what you can to meet monthly. This

will also give the supervisor the chance to give you feedback should you need to improve in any areas before the next time you are up for review.

11. Follow up. The best way to be remembered and get follow-through is to follow up. Follow up with everything! Call to confirm meetings, call to make sure people received the information you sent, and call to make sure your clients are happy. Let your clients, prospects, and contacts know you are out there and that you are thinking of them. A good example of why following up with people is so important are the several occasions I have gone to a lunch meeting to meet with a colleague or client and never gotten to eat, because they never showed up! People get busy, they forget, or something comes up. But I hate sitting in the waiting area alone, getting sympathetic looks from the hostess. Even worse, I had a lunch meeting a few years ago at one of the fanciest restaurants in town. When I entered, I was immediately ushered to a table, even though I said I was waiting for another person. After waiting for twenty minutes at my table, I decided to order. I was hungry and on a schedule, and I was sure my colleague would join me soon. Unfortunately though, I ended up eating by myself, which was bad enough at a nice restaurant, but several people I knew also came through the restaurant that day, including an ex-boyfriend, an old boss, and the mayor. "Hi Meg, eating alone?" I was so embarrassed that I am now extra prudent about these follow-up calls!

12. Smile for the camera! Have a good professional photo taken and consider putting that on your business cards, website, and/or company brochure. People will remember you more when they can put a face with a name.

13. Have a tagline. When you introduce yourself, use a tagline or a clever saying that will be remembered and will help others associate you with what you do.

14. Get networked. Join a networking group that will help you to promote yourself. Groups like BNI or the National Association of Women Business Owners (NAWBO) will help you to promote yourself and your business.

Self-promotion is important to reach the next levels of success, and it can be done tastefully and professionally. Look for opportunities, don't be afraid to ask for help, and remember to keep your ultimate goals in mind!

– ACTIVITY –
SELF-PROMOTION

Writing articles is one of the best ways to get noticed and recognized as an expert. Can you think of types of business magazines or papers for which you could write?

For this activity you will need some magazines and local newspapers, a pair of scissors, and tape. Go through the magazines and newspapers and clip out the names and contact information of the editors and the submission information and tape them into your notebook. Make notes about where they came from if necessary. Also clip any articles that may be of interest to you, along with the writer's name and contact information.

Add to these clippings as you find magazines to which you think you could contribute, and when you are ready, send an email with your manuscript or story ideas.

SELF-BRANDING—DEVELOPING THE OUTER YOU

Self-branding is a little different than self-promotion, although they have the same goal of getting you and your business more attention. By learning how to brand yourself, you will

- Increase your client base

- Demand more for your services (and salary)

- Spend less time and money marketing your product

- Become a recognized expert in your field

- Stand out from your coworkers and competition

- Continue to increase your success

Self-branding will differentiate you. You can go about self-branding by thinking of yourself as a product you need to market. What is your personal mission and vision? What kind of image do you want to portray? What is your message? What do you want people to remember after they meet you? After you meet someone, consider how you believe that he or she perceived you and work to refine that assessment.

As with any other kind of branding, your own self-branding needs to stay on message and be consistent and memorable. Incorporate the aspects of self-promotion (like having a tagline), learn how to tell your story, and express your opinion with your personal mission and vision in mind at all times.

CONFIDENCE—YOUR SECRET WEAPON

Are you a confident person? Do others see you as having confidence?

People, especially us introverted people, are complex and (sometimes overly) emotional beings. You may be a very confident person among your friends but then pull a wallflower routine at the office, just working on getting through every day to be able to go home and get back to your comfort zone.

Personal growth and success come from confidence. You are working to better yourself and to make a better life. The process alone will boost your confidence, but that is just the beginning! You are good at what you do, and you are a good person with expertise and abilities that are sought after. You deserve to be recognized.

> ## shy girl tip:
> ### Confidence
>
> A great way to gain confidence is to smile. You not only look more confident but also will feel it too!

I myself will never be an athlete; however, occasionally I do go to the gym, go snowboarding or cross-country skiing, shoot hoops with a friend, swim, or go for a little jog. I do this to build my confidence in sports and to get a little exercise. I want to have decent base knowledge and experience in different things—and it's good for me.

I also watch football; listen to pigheaded conservative radio talk-show hosts; ask my fifteen-year-old neighbor about her school classes; and go to scary, evil-machine-takes-over-the-world sci-fi movies to build my confidence and knowledge, and because it is good for me.

I do my hair, wear a good suit, prepare for meetings, print out driving directions, and research my prospect's company to build my confidence before a big presentation, and because it is good for me!

Confidence comes from knowing what you are doing, where you are going, and why you are there. Confidence will come to you when you are prepared, engaged, and ready to accept it. People are attracted to confidence, and when people are attracted to you, it will be easy to win them over, show them what you are about, and teach them about your product or the cause you are passionate about. You will gain support and positive business momentum because you believe in what you are doing and in yourself.

– ACTIVITY –
CONFIDENCE BUILDING

For this activity, you will need a good friend, relative, or spouse. Turn to a clean sheet in your notebook and on the top write your name. Then draw a line down the middle. On the left write, "Things (your name) is good at," and on the right side write, "Things (your name) is not so good at." Have your friend, spouse, or relative write the list of things that they believe, objectively, that you are good at. Then in the right-hand column dictate what you find challenging. For example:

Things Michelle is good at...	Things Michelle is not so good at...
Painting	Singing
Cooking	Spelling

Drawing	Math
Being generous	
Home repairs	
Organization	
Appreciating others	
Swimming	
Making people laugh	

You will see from this activity that you are good at many more things than not. But even if your right-hand column is longer than you would like, consider the value of these qualities. Are people going to dislike you because you aren't a great speller? Of course not. But they will like you more if you appreciate them and make them laugh.

Turn back to this page anytime you need a boost of confidence!

ROCK THAT BOAT—MAKING WAVES

The fact of the matter is that if you have spent your life trying not to stand out and not make any ripples, you are already at a severe disadvantage to those ripple-making type of people. To be successful, there are times when not only will you have to cause a bit of a ripple, you will have to learn how to cause some big waves too. Everything from your appearance to your résumé will have to stand out just a little more.

> ## shy girl tip:
> *Rocking the Boat*
>
> Go through your closet and pull out the outfit that is the most flattering on you. Match it with accessories and wear it the next day to work and see what happens.

If this idea scares you a little—good! You should have a bit of trepidation about doing something new or something different, but you can do it. The more you break through that initial fear each time you do something new, the more confident and successful you will be. As humans we get ourselves into habits because they are easy and comfortable. But being successful takes risks, pushing boundaries, and being open to new ideas.

No matter where you are in your career, you have the opportunity to become irresistible—irresistible to your peers, clients, boss, potential employers, and everyone else in your life!

We are all too often paralyzed by our routines. As a (rather silly and slightly embarrassing) example, I like black boots. So nearly every day for ten years, I wore black boots with almost everything. I wore black boots with jeans, suit pants, and khakis. I wore them to the mall, to work, and out for dinner. I had six pairs of nearly identical black boots. In short, it was comfortable (and I thought they just went with everything)!

And then one day I bought a beautiful purple pantsuit, and I needed another pair of shoes. I had to admit that black and that shade of purple just didn't work. So I went out and

I bought the cutest little dark platinum pumps. Yes it seems silly, but I loved those shoes. I realized that I loved those shoes as much as I did the black boots. I realized that there were other options out there that were just as good, maybe better—options that went better with many of my outfits and made more sense. My coworkers noticed too—not so much the shoes, but that I looked different. I looked "great." I received many compliments that platinum-pump day, on everything from my appearance to how well my work and self-confidence had improved. Who knew shoe shopping would be both liberating and professionally rewarding?

Inadvertently I had extended myself. I made a choice to go outside my comfort level, and I was rewarded for it. And I now have a closet full of very different, wonderful shoes—as well as a just a couple pairs of very nice black boots.

Here are some simple ways for you to start a bit of a ripple:

1. Dress up for work. Dress a little better than you normally would every day for two weeks. If you normally wear a T-shirt to work, wear a polo shirt or a blouse. If you wear khakis, wear a suit. Need ideas? Check out what your supervisors are wearing. It may seem like a cliché, but dressing up can serve only to elevate other's opinions of you. Keep a journal in your notepad to list the comments made and compliments given.

2. Invite your boss out to lunch. Invite your supervisor to lunch and try not to talk about the mundane, day-to-day work topics. Talk about new trends in the industry, an article you hope to get published, a snowboarding trip you have planned, or a charity event you are involved in. Tell your boss about your dreams and where you hope to be in ten years. Also ask your boss about his or her own goals and dreams. Make a personal connection if you have not had one before. This will make asking for a raise or getting feedback on a project later on all that much easier. It may even open a door that you didn't even know was there.

3. Bring in doughnuts or a snack for your coworkers. Everyone loves food, and this will certainly get you noticed. (And don't just leave an open box with a note on it in the break room. Announce that you brought food as you walk in, or send out an email to let everyone know.)

4. Schedule a meeting to discuss your long-term goals with your supervisor. Request an official one-on-one. Come prepared with a list of questions and supporting evidence. Keep the meeting on topic and on time. Ask for advice on how you can improve.

5. Get a haircut or buy a new outfit. Nothing builds confidence more than looking your best. Go splurge—invest in yourself! People will notice.

6. Rearrange your office furniture or organize your desk. Even subtle change of any kind will catch people's attention. Make your workspace a bit different, more interesting, neater, and more professional. Add a plant or piece of art. Little things sometimes make a big difference.

7. Learn something new about someone in your office you don't know well. Go out of your way to introduce yourself and get to know someone new. Try to seek out someone who is new to the company or your area. They too are likely looking for a new friend or contact and will bring no preconceived ideas about you to the relationship. Then go introduce that person to the rest of your team!

8. Volunteer. Volunteer to run the blood drive or host the company holiday party or lead a special charity team. Let people know that you are available, willing to participate, and excited to work with them on projects beyond work.

9. Remember important dates. Keep track of important dates and send cards or an email on birthdays, anniversaries, graduations, or just because. A simple note can go a long way to remind people not only that you are there but also that you care.

10. Get recognized elsewhere. Finding it difficult to get noticed at work? Concentrate on getting the praise and recognition you deserve outside of your company. I assure you that if a newspaper article is written about your accomplishments as the chair of a community event, you will attract attention.

Break from the routine, from the simplest things to the more challenging or elaborate. Try something new. Rock that boat!

MANAGEMENT—YOU ARE THE BOSS OF YOU

The introvert may learn to be a phenomenal public speaker, build a successful network, have career success, work a room, and walk with confidence, but let's be honest, it's exhausting! That is the difference between introverts and extroverts; extroverts gain energy from other people, and introverts feel like they just get the energy sucked out of them by other people. I literally feel like I lose something of myself when I am obligated to chat with someone with whom I honestly don't wish to speak. This is especially true in situations that are new, unplanned, or involve a lot of people. And that is why, in certain public situations, you must manage yourself, or choose what is beneficial and energizing.

You do not need to be on all the time. In fact, if it is not your natural self to be outgoing, then it is profoundly important not to talk to every person you sit next to on a plane or to make cell phone calls every time you get into your car. You need to take time for yourself, by yourself.

If you are doing a special event, leading a big meeting, or doing a speech, take time to walk or read before and after. Close the door to your office. Relax with a friend. Being an introvert is not something to overcome or change—but it is something to be aware of and to manage. Acknowledge that you may need to balance your new, more outwardly outgoing self with a quieter, more introspective personality. Keep balance in mind, and you'll get the most out of the time you spend charming the public.

MENTOR AND BE MENTORED

As much as we may want a steadfast set of directions to reach the top in our careers, make our first million dollars, or lead a fulfilling life, there is no one way that that works for everyone. Life does, however, give us guides in the form of mentors; people whose behavior, success, attitude, or career we wish to emulate. Mentors can assist you in determining your goals, meeting the right people, working through your roadblocks, and celebrating with you when you reach your milestones.

Throughout your life, you will find people who will be informal mentors. You will learn from and confide in them. You may not even realize that they are mentors until long after they have affected your life or career. You may also be assigned a formal mentor through your company or organization. There is no limit to the number of mentors you can have, formal or informal. Reach out to the people who are living the kind of life that you would like to lead, and take advantage of opportunities to bring positive, interesting, motivational people into your life.

Finding and interacting with a mentor may be a bit awkward for the introvert. Asking for help may not come easily, so here are some steps for starting a mentoring relationship:

1. Ask close friends or coworkers about themselves, who they look up to, or how they got to where they are in business. By asking questions of someone you already feel comfortable with, you will learn how to ask the same of a new mentor. And in the process, you may find valuable insight from someone you already know.

2. After taking the extra time and learning about several of your close friends and coworkers, tell them you would like to meet with someone they admire or consider a mentor. This can be a very casual meeting with the three of you. Ask the same types of questions of their mentor that you asked your friend, and remember to offer some of your own story and why you are interested in speaking with them (i.e., because he or she is in a similar industry, has a similar background, or was particularly successful).

3. Practice makes perfect, so continue to learn more about the people you have known well and for a long time, stay in touch with their mentors, and begin to look for other people whom you admire and whose lives you would like to emulate.

4. Once you have identified a person or two whom you would like to consider for your mentor, send a note or an email requesting a meeting. Remember that they may be busy and may not respond to your request. This doesn't make them not worth learning from, but it may take them out of the good-mentor category.

5. When you identify a good mentor and he or she has agreed to have an initial meeting with you, keep the meeting focused, ask prepared questions, and listen intently. If you find the meeting valuable, ask if your new mentor would mind if you kept in touch. If he or she says yes, remember the importance of follow-up.

One of the most rewarding things that you can do is to be a mentor yourself. Do this by leading by example, living an exemplary life, and striving to do better. Volunteer to be a mentor or recognize when a friend, contact, or colleague can benefit from your experience, advice, and perspective. The best way to be a good mentor is to listen, take your time, and help others come to their own conclusions, to assist without doing the job for them.

Introverts may tend to reject the idea of mentorship at the outset. It isn't easy to ask for help or request that someone take you under his or her wing. It may be even more difficult to commit to doing the same for another person. However, introverts need mentor relationships more than extroverts because they naturally keep a tighter circle of friends and associates. Mentors can help the introvert with introductions and in gaining confidence in speaking to new people. As a mentor you can learn from someone new, with a fresh perspective, as well as teach, listen, coach, and be a guide as someone else's success becomes yours as well.

LEARNING FROM THE BEST—THE WEGMANS APPROACH

The summer after my sixteenth birthday, I went down to the local grocery store to apply for a job. It was my first interview, my first real job, my first experience with the corporate world, and my first taste of true independence.

The excitement of a potential job just barely overrode the nearly paralyzing fear of starting something new, with new people, in a new place. I sat down in the HR manager's office the day of my interview, and I remember that she immediately made feel welcome and comfortable. The ease with which she spoke to me and made me relax was not lost on me, even at such a young age. This was the first of many experiences that I had with how well run Wegmans was and is. I was not treated as a shy child looking for summer employment but as an adult interviewing for a job. After being offered and accepting a position in the bulk-foods department, I was sent to training and taught about corporate culture, customer service, store policies, and the company history. By the time I started working in the store, I already felt like I was a part of the team.

Choosing Wegmans as my first employer was an easy decision, and I am grateful they chose me. They had a location within walking distance; they were known for being efficient and generous to their employees in terms of pay and benefits, even to part-time employees; and they had a reputation for providing first-rate training. As a first job, Wegmans made a very positive impression on me as to how a quality business should operate.

My department supervisor at Wegmans was the kind of person who always had a kind word to say and remembered everyone's birthdays. Norma genuinely cared for each employee and was a natural leader with her strong presence, patience, and gentle guidance. Norma knew how to train, motivate, and inspire each of her employees and the people around her. I thrived as Norma's employee. She was my first mentor and a hardworking, knowledgeable leader. Wegmans is full of people like Norma (although none quite as truly wonderful).

The company grew from a single produce cart to a multi-state grocery powerhouse, and the company continues to excel through a commitment to employees. Their focus on the individual employee allowed me, the introvert, to develop my first business skills. I received the personal attention I needed to feel important and was brought into new areas of the business and given responsibility as I gained more experience. Wegmans had a commitment to making me a better employee and giving me the skills I needed to be successful as an employee and in life.

Throughout my years at Wegmans, I was educated and mentored. From the application process to the training I received, my managers, and the scholarship I was awarded, Wegmans showed me how a good company should function. It is now, with many years of perspective, that I can tell you that some of the best business lessons I've ever learned, I learned in my first job at a grocery store, an incredibly well-run business, and from the people who worked there.

Supported by thousands in the corporate offices, warehouses, bakeries, and farms, Wegmans stores are as unique as their commitment to their team. Wegmans is not just an average grocery store; it is a marvelous total shopping experience, and some stores offer everything from gourmet chocolate to a sushi bar. Wegmans has thought of everything a consumer might want and delivers it in a beautiful setting that makes it hard for the shopper to do anything but slowly stroll, taking in the smells and architecture while sipping on their $3 latte and piling their carts full of wonderful food and groceries. (And this is the reason I hardly go into Wegmans at all anymore; the space-time continuum does not exist in those buildings, and I can lose hours!)

The Wegmans shoppers love it. They love spending time in the stores. They love taking the time to shop, and they love being made to feel special. It is not uncommon for visitors to Rochester, New York, to get a tour from a proud resident of one or more of the bigger Wegmans stores. It is that unique!

The combination of well-trained, intelligent, knowledgeable, happy employees and world-class products in an inviting environment makes them the envy of other grocery stores and other businesses worldwide. It is no wonder they have been recognized with countless awards including *Fast Company* magazine's Employee Innovator Award (October 2004), and *Fortune's* 100 Best Companies to Work For every year since it was first published in 1998 and has ranked among the top ten for six consecutive years. Respect and reward employees, train top-notch managers, create a unique and rewarding experience for clients, and promote an environment for personal accountability and learning—Wegmans gave me all of these lessons and continues to exemplify how to be a successful company and how to create successful businesspeople.

– ACTIVITY –
LOOKING FOR LESSONS

My experience with Wegmans was rewarding on many levels, as I learned about a well-run business.

On a fresh sheet in your notebook, list the companies you have worked for that you feel do business at the highest level of their industry. On each line, after the company name, write just one characteristic that describes it. Use words like *customer service, commitment, quality.*

Think about what can be gleaned from their best practices and how you can extract lessons from your interactions with these top performers. How can you apply this to your life and business?

Chapter 5
Advanced Business Knowledge

Once you have established yourself in your career, gained confidence, self-promoted, rocked the boat, been a mentor and been mentored, and learned from the best, you have established a base from which to be great—but you have still just begun your journey toward success.

There is so much more that has to be done to be truly successful in business. The qualities and habits of the really successful can be learned, reproduced, and incorporated into anyone's life. True success is a desire to continue learning, the ability to accept that which you cannot change, and the drive to work a little harder to reach your goals.

HAVE A BACKUP PLAN (AND WHY I ALWAYS CARRY A TEA BAG)

At age seventeen, I traveled from my moderately middle-class, rather boring upstate New York home to Belfast, Northern Ireland. Long known for its troubles, Northern

Ireland is officially part of Great Britain, even though it sits at the tip of Ireland. This tiny place has seen more than its fair share of hardships.

I went to Northern Ireland to spend two weeks in the city of Belfast with longtime family friends. During my stay I witnessed, for the first time in my life, bombings, deplorable living conditions, and the tragedies of a senseless war, and I learned enough unforgettable life lessons to fill a book of its own.

My great-aunt lived in the South of Ireland, in a town called Bantry (on the nearly opposite end of the isle from Belfast), but she had said on a dozen different occasions that if I ever found myself in Ireland to look her up and come "stop in any time" for a visit.

Now, I wasn't about to drop in unannounced on a relative on a completely different continent from my own, so I decided to contact my aunt. But Aunt Pauline did not have a phone in her house, so about a month before I left for Ireland, I sent a letter to her telling her that I wished to visit and to contact us if she, for whatever reason, did not wish me to come. In the letter I included contact information for both my own family and the family with which I was staying in the North.

I didn't expect to hear from my aunt. Long-distance phone calls were expensive and the closest public telephone was in town, quite a distance from her house. My parents and I assumed that she would write or call if there was a reason for me not to come. We took it on faith that my great-aunt meant what she had said in so many invitations, and that any time meant any time.

My journey from Belfast to Bantry was long and tiring. We took plenty of taxis and trains and buses. It took three days and nights to travel all the way south. They were three awful days with no sleep and tired feet, and we had only about forty dollars to buy transportation and food and traverse an entire country. It was not the glamorous backpacking-through-Europe trip by any stretch of the imagination.

When we arrived, it was pouring rain, and my aunt was not there when two weary, soaking-wet kids got off the bus and stepped into the then-flooded streets of Bantry. She had not been in town to meet us when we got off the bus, nor was she home when we finally found her tiny rustic hillside cottage. Aunt Pauline was obviously not expecting me. My best friend was furious that I had dragged her to this place with no shelter and no family to take us in. We were broke, wet, cold, and essentially lost. Sunlight was disappearing rapidly, and we had nothing to do but sit on her step and wait. We had no backup plan.

Fortunately, after hours of sitting in the rain, silently bemoaning our situation on Aunt Pauline's front step, the elderly couple who had been peering out from behind their draperies next door finally came out to investigate in person the soaked strangers. With their thick country accents and their ancient leathery hands, they guided us into their little cottage home. The pair hurriedly placed space heaters around us and pealed away our wet coats. They brought us sandwiches and cookies and the

shy girl tip:

Backup Plan

Carry something with you that will always make you feel more confident or comfortable. Consider a picture of a loved one, a contact list, or a note with your mission statement written on it.

most glorious, delicious cup of hot tea I have ever had.

We sat there for hours making polite conversation and watching out the window for my missing aunt Pauline. Finally, late into the night, the old man ushered my confused aunt into the couple's home. The woman gazed upon me with hardly any sense of recognition or understanding of the unusual situation. My cheeks flushed and my heart sank that last bit, as I realized that even as she began to recognize who I was, it was clear that she was not delighted to see me.

I had gone to see my aunt Pauline in Ireland for a lot of reasons. She was a link to a deceased grandmother whom I missed dearly, and she was family in a faraway place that was sometimes lonely and very scary for me. What I got out of the experience was different—but still valuable. I learned that when traveling through life or foreign countries, you should always have a little extra cash, a ready change of clothes, and a tea bag to make a nice hot pot of tea.

It was the hot tea that we drank along the way at the cafés and bus stations that nourished and sustained us for those three days. It gave us strength, and it warmed and soothed us that night in the kind strangers' home.

Believe me, that trip was not a success. It is, however, a metaphor for the journey of life in which we all partake. Sometimes you go on a search for answers to burning questions or a feeling of connection in a faraway land. Sometimes your search is for ways to manage introversion, for the perfect job, for recognition, or for love. But life has a strange way of giving us what we need and not always what we want. Sometimes that is an incredible gift, and sometimes the success is in recognizing that unexpected gift.

ESTABLISH YOURSELF AS AN EXPERT

One of the best ways to become an undeniable success in your career is to be an expert. Your expertise will open new doors for you, introduce you to new people and opportunities, and propel you to a whole new level.

Experts are respected and sought after; they attract others, and they can bring excitement to conferences, businesses, and events. If you are an established expert in your field, the media will come to you, you will be sought out for interviews, and you will be more attractive to your current and prospective employer. Establishing yourself as an expert is not as difficult as you might think and can go a long way to make you more marketable, more fulfilled, and more sought after.

If you are passionate about what you do and dedicated to being the best at it, becoming an expert is a very obtainable goal. Generally it takes only about seven years of dedicated focus on a subject matter to become an expert, but there are several fields that require more time (such as in the technology-driven industries, medical fields, or the sciences). Think about the time you have already invested in your knowledge base, the things that you excel at, and decide whether you are or can become an expert in this subject matter.

After gaining the expertise, you will need to get the word out that you are the premier resource on the subject. Being a recognized expert is not so much what you know, but who knows that you know what you know. There are many ways to become an established expert, but often the best way to be great is to seek great recognition.

CONTINUING EDUCATION

Whether you are an introvert or an extrovert, it is easy to get complacent. We get complacent in our personal lives and in our professional lives. We forget to be persistent, to keep our goals in mind, and to move forward and continuously seek challenges. Sometimes investing in ourselves, by learning more and staying current with technology and industry trends, gets put on a back burner. Success and happiness do not, however, shine on the complacent. Success comes when we try a little harder, do a little more, and open ourselves up to learning opportunities.

Taking classes and being a student are not my favorite things. It isn't the learning or the extra work that I cringe at; it is being in a room for days or weeks or months on end with a bunch of people I would not have chosen to surround myself with. I feel trapped and uncomfortable, and this often affects my ability to learn. As an introvert, I am not drawn to a classroom setting, but that doesn't mean I don't think it is vitally important to keep learning. When I don't feel comfortable, I can't expect to learn as well. That means that I sometimes have to look for ways to get this education in a way that is more in sync with my personality, such as online webinars or tele-seminars. When these are not available, I look for ways to make the traditional class easier for me. I make sure that I have quiet time before and after, and I go with a friend if possible.

It is very important, in the quest for success, to keep up to date and to refine the skills that will assist us in our greatness. But it is most important to realize that the more we get out and learn about ourselves and about our specialties, the closer we are to being a true success.

One of the best examples of how continuing education paid off for me happened a couple of years ago. I went to a seminar about search engine optimization, which admittedly puts the majority of the population into an immediate sleepy stupor but is still one of my absolute favorite topics. I look for opportunities to learn as much about search engine optimization as I can. Furthermore, a competitor was hosting the seminar, and it is always good to know everything your competition knows (and more).

At the seminar, I sat next to a delightful woman who, during the break, asked me if I had understood what the last speaker had said. I apparently impressed her so much with my answer explaining page rank that she told me that I was the one who should have been giving the seminar. She and the company she represented became very lucrative clients for my company. I learned some new ideas about Internet marketing and picked up an outstanding customer in the process.

Attending seminars, taking online courses, finishing up a degree, or going for that next level of competency is an important and vital ingredient in your success. The benefits will go above and beyond stretching your brain, new clients, a new opportunity, better compensation, and being more efficient and effective in your job.

CHARISMA

A large part of success is being irresistible. It is about having a charisma that draws people to you. The beauty of charisma is that it does the hard work for introverts—it takes the pressure off going to people because they come to you. Yet just the thought of trying to be charismatic, and therefore noticed, is more than a little daunting for the introvert. But relax! You can be quietly irresistible in a way that is subtle, yet undeniable.

Being charismatic is about being attractive, and being attractive is about more than just physical appearance—it is

---

shy girl tip:

Charisma

One of the most irresistible things about people is their friendliness—so make eye contact and be open to those around you.

about how you carry yourself, how you speak, and what you have to say. If you are charismatic, those around you will not have the choice of whether or not to be attracted; they just will be.

First, give yourself permission. Say, "I give myself permission to be a charismatic person who draws people to me because of my knowledge, experience, presence, and ability to convey my message." Remove any negative feelings or trepidation you have about the attention this may bestow on you. Embrace it. You are worth the attention.

Here are a few ways to start thinking positively about the attention you receive.

• Think about times when getting attention gave you a positive feeling, such as recognition at work, a birthday, or a wedding.

• Think about how it would feel to have your picture in the paper or to receive an award.

• Think about what impressive things you will accomplish when you are able to garner more attention.

Second, think about what attracts you to others—seemingly effortless effectiveness, easy conversation, intelligence, and confidence. Strive to emulate people to whom you are attracted. We are attracted to people who are great because they make being great look easy. So take a deep breath, be good at what you do, and practice talking about your area of expertise until it does, finally, become easy.

Unfortunately, the thing about trying to be charismatic is that sometimes, the harder you try, the less successful you will be. Nothing is more unattractive than the person who seems like they are trying too hard. So, if you feel like you are trying too hard, you probably are. Take the time to learn by observing others and focusing on the smaller ways to show your charisma at first (such as how you talk about yourself and your ability to make others feel comfortable around you). Then slowly start incorporating these things into your everyday life. Be patient and aware of how you are perceived. Your comfort and confidence in your area of expertise will show on the outside and make you more charismatic to the people around you.

TAKING THE LEAD

The first step in becoming an irresistible success at work is to take the lead. Whatever level you are at or aspire to reach, you can obtain leadership.

Leaders provide direction to a group of individuals working toward a common goal, but leadership is a very intangible ability. While the characteristics of a good leader may be hard to define, there are concrete and real qualities that all leaders possess. These qualities separate the good from the great.

Below are ten methods that can assist you in taking the lead. These habits transcend industries and job titles.

1. Extend yourself. Become a mentor to a student or new employee. Teach them what you know and counsel them on ways to improve. As others see that you can be a confident mentor and teacher, you will be given additional responsibility.

2. Open up to opportunities. As an effective leader, you should be accessible and approachable. Make a point of being available to anyone in search of your assistance.

3. Share the credit, and take the blame. If you are recognized for your brilliant work, remember to graciously accept the praise, and make sure that others involved in the project receive recognition as well. However, as the leader, it is your responsibility to shoulder the blame should something not go right.

4. Speak well, be polite, and be clear. One of the hardest things to learn is how and when to say the right thing. We each have different standards on what "right" is. However, understanding what is proper and appropriate in different circumstances, with different people, is critical to being a great leader. Be positive, pay attention, and connect. Learn to accept compliments.

5. Be grateful. Thank others when appropriate, and show your appreciation on a job well done. When people feel good about their contributions, they will be more likely to want to work well for you in the future.

6. Get to know them. Get to know the people you interact with every day: your peers, coworkers, supervisors, and employees. Say hello to them in the hall, ask how they are doing, and send cards and letters. Leaders make a point of learning about others so that they can best use their skills and interests (and it could brighten someone's day).

7. Relax and be flexible. Having the goal of being a great leader is fantastic, but it takes time and sometimes comes in unexpected ways. Leaders recognize opportunities, consult others, and are flexible.

8. Take the lead. One of the greatest qualities that a leader can possess is initiative. To be a great leader, you must show initiative to get the job done. Take the lead. Do not wait to be given leadership. Be the leader.

9. Be positive. Be sure to make the people you work with feel good about working with you. Make everyone feel important.

10. Get back in a timely fashion. Return email, phone calls, and so on. The longer you lag in getting back to your clients, vendors, and coworkers, the more likely your team is to do the same.

Being a great and effective leader takes practice and a lot of common sense. You can develop your leadership skills and transform your life.

BEING A GREAT LEADER

It is one thing to be a leader and a better thing to be a great leader.

> **shy girl tip:**
> *Great Leadership*
>
> Recognize the great leaders in your life—parents, teachers, friends—and emulate the things you admire in them.

And yet the skills of a great leader may not come naturally to you as an introvert. You can learn all of the basic skills of taking the lead, but as an introvert, to go one step further and become great, you need to have a true passion. Great leadership takes all of the general leader characteristics and brings them to the next level. Great leaders demand respect and are charismatic and ambitious—and this is because they are passionate about what they do. The introvert-leader is one whose passion for the job, work, or business enables him or her to excel in an area that would not otherwise come naturally. Great leaders love what they do, and great leaders are in tune with the people around them and the community in which they live and work.

True, effective leaders, in Congress or at the reception desk, have cultivated and demonstrated adeptness in the basics of leadership that long outlasts the more dramatic and self-serving. Most people know when they're in the presence of a real leader, real brilliance, and real proficiency—because it is palpable.

How does this true leadership show itself? As with so much, a great leader's passion will show itself and allow that individual to step outside of him- or herself, away from fears and insecurities, and find a way to leave each person that he or she has contact with feeling a little better. They may not be even formally recognized as leaders, but they choose to demonstrate their leadership skills not because their job demands it, but rather as a conscious decision to live an exemplary life.

Great leaders:

- Are focused on where they are, what they are doing, and to whom they are speaking

- Understand the power of their words and actions, and are mindful of the effect on others

- Are positive, always encouraging those around them to take on challenges, seek success, and live their dreams

- Are humble, never letting their own ego cloud their capacity to lead

- Are honest, speak the truth in private and public, and uphold the moral and ethical standards of their profession

- Persevere, accept risks and challenges knowing that they may stumble, and are able to keep moving

- Are courageous—fear and uncertainty will always be present, but great leaders push through and pursue their goals

- Are thoughtful, keep up on communications, say "hello," show appreciation, and give praise as appropriate

These are just some ways a great leader goes above and beyond, regardless of his or her official job title or capacity. Think about the leadership qualities you already have and the ways you are already a leader. What opportunities for leadership have passed you by? What opportunities do you have right now? The reward of true leadership is that it will continue to grow as you grow, and the opportunities to lead will always exist.

SEEKING OUT FEEDBACK

Asking for feedback is not always easy. It is, however, sometimes necessary. If you are not surrounded by people who naturally and frequently tell you when you are doing an excellent job and offer you unsolicited advice, you will have to ask.

Getting feedback will make you more effective and help you develop your leadership, communication, and networking skills. Asking for feedback will also break the feelings of isolation you may feel and give you further confidence in your interaction with others.

Maybe you have asked for feedback before and it has been negative or unhelpful. Don't be intimidated or let this stop you from seeking it out again; just ask someone else.

Find the people who offer the best constructive criticism and graciously disregard the advice or feedback of negative individuals. You will begin to build and strengthen a circle of people whom you can trust for good feedback on all subjects.

Perhaps you are afraid to take up too much of another person's time when asking for feedback. In general, people will be happy to tell you what they thought about a project you did or your performance if asked. People like to be asked for their opinion and be consulted on areas that are obviously important to you. If they are unable to or uninterested in devoting a few minutes and giving you that attention, they will probably tell you. As long as you don't abuse the goodwill of others by going to them frequently, you are likely not a bother at all.

The last excuse people often use for shying away from asking for feedback is that they don't know how to ask. My answer—just ask. If it doesn't come out right or you don't get the reaction you are looking for, ask someone else in a different way. Keep learning, practicing, and asking. Without the risk there is no reward.

CAPITALIZE ON OPPORTUNITIES

Sometimes the best opportunities happen at the most inopportune times, but that doesn't mean you shouldn't take them anyway.

Last year I was asked to do a radio interview about how technology has changed our lives in the past thirty years, and I was very excited to have that opportunity. It was the second time I had been asked to be on that particular show (the first interview focused on the "third" Industrial Revolution—which, I know, can be a pretty boring subject but is still one of my favorites). I felt relaxed with the interviewer, and of course I was very interested in the topic. After so many years of hiding from publicity, I was finally almost comfortable with the process. I have found that radio interviews are pretty easy for me. They are low-key—like talking to a friend, and usually they send you the main points ahead of time, so you can prepare. I definitely recommend this for the publicity-hungry introvert!

So, I scheduled the interview and began to think about all of the intelligent, witty, articulate things I could say about technology. Then I realized that I was going to be on vacation that week, and I wouldn't be able to do the interview. I was very disappointed.

I knew I wanted to do the radio show, and so, after agonizing about what to do, I eventually got up the courage and asked the producer if we could set up a telephone interview—and they said it was no problem. To be honest, I never would have asked before, but because I really wanted to do the interview, I stepped out of my comfort zone and onto that proverbial limb. Apparently, phone interviews were something the station did all the time, so even though it was a big request for me, it was an easy concession for them to grant.

Since then I have grabbed at each promotional opportunity I could, doing several newspaper interviews via cell phone while commuting, including one while in line at the Safari in Disney World and another for a radio show while pushing my sleeping baby in the stroller, pacing behind a rack of G-strings at Victoria's Secret and waving off the helpful sales girl (the interviewer called my cell phone: I wasn't going to tell them I wasn't available, even if I was shopping for underwear!).

The point is, sometimes the best opportunities are thrown at you, sometimes they will bend for you, and sometimes you will have to bend for them. Embrace the challenges, the irony, the hilarity, and the shear chaos that these events force upon your life, and take that opportunity!

GETTING PROFESSIONAL HELP

Sometimes you may need to ask for professional help. Not the medical kind (although this too can be helpful), but the kind of help that you get from quality professional services. The sign of a true leader and successful person is the ability to recognize when help is needed. No matter how strong your friends are and how much you may shy away from the idea of reaching beyond your immediate circle of associates, it is best sometimes to go to a professional.

There are many options available depending on what areas in your life you feel have room for improvement. I have used professional coaches, sales trainers, a publicist, a professional bio writer, recruiters, and a personal assistant. Before finishing this book, I will use the services of a professional editor. I know that I am not perfect at everything and that sometimes I need a little extra help to learn and grow and accomplish or to supplement the work that I am doing.

> **shy girl tip:**
> *How to Ask*
>
> If asking for help is difficult, begin the conversation by asking what you can do for someone else. Your genuine interest in helping someone else will often prompt the other person to ask what he or she can do for you!

It is the job of these professionals to make you better, to teach you, to train you, and to challenge you. Often these people see your greatness and potential for success before you do.

Still need convincing? Tiger Woods has a coach, a caddy, and a whole team of advisers making sure he succeeds. Lance Armstrong has a crew of people who follow him around, provide medical attention, keep his water bottles filled and his bicycles tuned up and ready to go, and a whole team of advisers making sure he succeeds. The president of the United States has a cabinet, a vice president, and a whole team of advisers and staff making sure he succeeds. Oprah Winfrey has producers, writers, consultants, stylists, and a whole team of advisers making sure she succeeds. You deserve to have a team looking out for you and making sure that you always present yourself in the best way.

Asking for help can be a little intimidating; however, it is necessary to recognize the benefits of professional help and to use it.

Chapter 6
Business Networking

Business networking is vital to the introvert's business success. Being tremendous at networking will mean the difference between getting by and making a huge impact. For the introvert, business networking will open up the doors that need opening, keep you off the phone on those dreaded cold calls, and keep you at the top of the minds of your network.

THE IMPORTANCE OF NETWORKING

It is hard to explain the importance of business networking to someone who has never given it much thought. Meeting new people, strengthening alliances, and growing your business is meaningless to a person who has never looked at his or her address book as anything other than names and addresses of family, friends, the doctor, and the baby-sitter. However, once you begin to see that networking is rewarding both personally and professionally, the benefits of networking are nearly limitless.

Here are some excellent reasons to network:

1. Very often, people choose where to do business on the basis of the recommendations of their friends, family, and trusted coworkers.

2. Any contact, such as a phone call or an email, to a potential client is much more compelling if you can make a personal connection ("Kelly Jones suggested I call").

3. To be a successful salesperson, you need to grow your prospects, and because you likely cannot meet every potential client for your business in person, you can instead spend the time to make good networking connections, which will result in many new clients.

4. When you refer your clients to businesses in your network, you are helping your clients, who get the products and services they need, and the businesses you refer them to, which in turn get new customers. This also strengthens your own relationship with your clients and your network.

5. By introducing two people, you increase their networks, thus increasing their potential for business and ultimately yours as well.

NETWORKING 101

Depending on your background, profession, location, and needs, *networking* will mean something unique to you. Whatever that is, you will ultimately find networking to be profoundly rewarding.

As an introvert, you have an advantage and natural strength in networking. While introverts may not make as many contacts, they tend to make stronger relationships with the contacts they do have. Remember that it is easier to nurture a relationship than to start a new one. Introverts naturally foster excellent, long-term networks.

I would rather have one hundred really great contacts, many of whom I consider friends, all of whom I could count on in a tough situation, than one thousand names in a card file who wouldn't recognize my name or go out of their way to help me out. Wouldn't you?

ASSESSING YOUR NETWORKING NEEDS

Your first step in this process is to assess your needs. What do you want to get out of networking? Do you need to network to grow your business, make more sales, meet more people, be a resource to your clients, get a promotion, or find a new job? Or all of the above?

For some, networking is purely social. As an introvert, it is unlikely that you have picked up this book just because you want to make more friends. (It is possible and likely, however, that through this process you will make many new friends.) It is much more likely that you have a strong desire to build your business network, but either you don't know where to start or you have stagnated and need to continue to grow your circle of influence.

The good news is you already have a network. You have friends, coworkers, contacts, and family. These people are your network. And each of these people has a network. Throughout the chapters of this book you will learn to leverage these contacts, and that is what makes networking work.

Furthermore, you already have the skills to network. You learned most of them before you were eight! Networking is merely meeting with new people and connecting with those you already know to further a mutually beneficial relationship. You have made friends before, you know how to have a pleasant conversation, and you have (at least you should have) sent thank-you notes before. You are well on your way! The hardest part of networking is building a strategy to make this valuable, following through, and being consistent.

Like most things of value in this world, networking is a journey—one you get to make with people you like and want to spend more time with.

What could be better than that?

FINDING YOUR STYLE

To begin the process of networking, you will need to recognize your networking style. For me, this was easy. I hate large groups and informal gatherings (you may love them and dislike structured groups). I avoid noisy gatherings and know that I do best when I can talk to people one-on-one. I also know that I am more comfortable talking to people when I have something in my hand—preferably a cup of hot tea (it might sound crazy, but it relaxes me and gives me something to focus on if my mind starts to wander). I know that I am more comfortable sitting in a coffee shop than I am at someone else's office—but my office will usually do, too, as long as there isn't much going on that day.

It took me a while to realize all of these things about myself, but they were all parts of my personality long before I ever knew about business networking.

YOU ALREADY HAVE THE SKILLS—APPLY THEM

Applying the things that you already know about yourself and applying the skills that you learned at an early age is just about all there is to networking. Watch any kindergarten class and you will see networking in action. Children naturally and easily make friends, share information, and build networks.

There is nothing about networking that is difficult per se. However, successful networking is a continual process, one that needs to be cultivated and fine-tuned. Networking should become part of your everyday routine, and it should be something that you are constantly willing and working to improve.

Building a successful network is as easy as remembering the things that you learned in kindergarten:

introduce yourself, share, be fair, take turns, play nice, and sometimes bring a snack!

MAKE NETWORKING YOUR JOB

To be a successful networker, whether introvert or extrovert, you may need to change your thinking. Effective networking doesn't happen in your spare time, and it is not something that can be deprioritized or put off until tomorrow. Networking must be part of your everyday life, and most important, part of your job, no matter what your job is.

> ## shy girl tip:
> *Networking*
>
> • Be genuine, smile, and be yourself.
> • Always look for opportunities to connect with other people.
> • Ask open-ended questions that will keep the conversation moving.
> • Know what you are looking for from the event or meeting.
> • Follow through with these people afterward.

Putting yourself out there to network can be overwhelming. The thing that makes networking challenging is not the steps that go into it but the fact that you will have to expose yourself, even just a little bit, to people and that can occasionally be a little intimidating for the introvert. It can be a little too easy not to send that email or make that call when confronted with the thought of interacting with someone new. Unfortunately, procrastination is natural when it comes to that which is least comfortable to us. You can't let this happen to networking.

It is very helpful to set up easy-to-achieve goals for yourself, because it is likely that no one else, even your boss, will set these networking goals for you.

Here are some easy ideas for the introvert to ease into thinking and living business networking as your job.

1. Go to one meeting per week with someone you have recently met and wish to get to know better.

2. Go to one meeting per week with someone who is important to your business.

3. Send a request for a meeting to at least five new people per week. (I like to send cards or email, as I am particularly shy with strangers on the phone.) Not everyone will respond, but this will help you line up meetings for the next few weeks easily.

4. Set up a meeting for the next week with someone who is important to your business. This should be very easy to set up, as you should be contacting these people regularly.

5. Once a month, set and attend a meeting with one person in your wider network.

6. Attend one networking meeting per week.

7. Attend one additional networking meeting or event per month.

8. Watch the lists of top performers and award winners and nominees in your local business publications, and put these on your contact wish list. Ask your existing contacts whether they know these people and try to add them to your network.

9. Send out thank-you cards to everyone you meet. Include a business card with every note.

Once this becomes routine, you will begin to feel more comfortable with networking. You will also begin to realize that you are quickly building your network, and that even though it is part of your job, it is actually fun and interesting to meet regularly with a wide variety of people.

REAP THE REWARDS OF BUSINESS NETWORKING

Networking is simultaneously the most undeniably effective kind of marketing and one of the hardest to measure in terms of effectiveness. However, there are real reasons that networking (also known as relationship marketing) is valuable to you. Your ability to recognize the effectiveness of your efforts will allow you to discover its benefits.

Here are six reasons that relationship marketing is the best way to build your business:

1. No more cold-calling. After you build a strong network, you will have to call only the people who you know you want to talk to or have been referred to.

2. Referral business. You will have a potential endless stream of referral business.

3. Be a resource. Help out your friends, family, clients, and other contacts when they are looking for something through your network.

4. Get an easy testimonial. You will have people who will give you a testimonial or reference for your business or for you personally.

5. A group of trusted advisers. You will have a group of people who can help you when you need a favor, feedback, or a new perspective.

6. A team of salespeople. You will have a group of people who will be thinking of you every time they meet someone new who expresses an interest in your area(s) of specialty and who will be able to refer your business.

GETTING MORE REFERRALS

The question of how to get more referrals is a very important one. You may meet with dozens of people a week, and they may become great friends, but unless you know how to parlay those relationships into business for you or your company, you won't get many referrals.

Sometimes asking for something is the hardest part of a conversation. We are programmed, for whatever reason, not to ask too much of people. But if you don't ask, it is unlikely that you will get—so you have to know how to ask for the help or for that referral.

Most people will want to help you. Helping is natural even if asking is not. By giving someone an idea of how to help, you make them feel better and make it easier for him or her to help you. Take, for example, the convenience of wedding-gift registries. Now you can decide not to get your sister the china she registered for but at least you know what pattern she picked out if you do.

There are ways to ask for a referral that are more correct than others. Always know ahead of time what a good referral would be for you. One of the worst feelings in the world is having someone who wants to help you, knowing you need help, but not knowing where to begin, how to ask, or what to ask for.

When meeting with someone, telling them what you want from them right off the bat is obviously not how you should start the conversation. Unless you have set up the meeting to discuss a particular project, always try to focus the first portion of the meeting on the other person. Ask your colleague or friend how he or she has been, what any new and interesting current projects are, and if there is anything you can do for him or her. Stay relaxed and let the conversation flow. There will be a natural opening for you to talk about what you are seeking. Ask specifics such as, "Do you know anyone at SCA Grocery? I have been trying to get in there to talk to their buyer." Or tell your new contact something about you, such as, "We have just opened our new line of natural breath mints. I would appreciate it if you run into anyone in the market for organic mouth-care products that you think of me and give them my card. We sell a full line of products such as sprays, mints, and food seasonings; it is some pretty amazing stuff." Remember that you aren't trying to sell to the person you are meeting with; you are building a network, a network of people who need to see you in the best-possible light, trust you, and think of you when they run into someone who may just be in the market for natural breath mints. Give them enough information to get them interested and to keep you in their minds if they encounter a referral opportunity.

The best advice I can give anyone looking to get more referrals is to ask. Ask and explain. Ask for what you want, be specific, and explain why you think that target would benefit.

In one networking group, we each have an opportunity to say what kinds of prospects we are seeking each week. I used to ask for "any business that wants a new website." I think partly this was because it was easy to remember. I could say that and just sit down. It wouldn't cause anyone to take any special notice of me. The problem was that that garnered very few results in terms of referrals. It was forgettable.

People need specifics, and they need you to give them the tools to assist you. For example, a chiropractor who asks for referrals for anyone with a back will get a few referrals, even though we all have a back, and he should theoretically have about five billion referrals. However, another chiropractor who says, "Migraines have been shown to be relieved and their frequency reduced by chiropractic adjustments, so anyone suffering through migraine headaches would be a good referral for me," will get five times the referrals of the first chiropractor.

Ask for the referral, be specific, and give a good reason why your product or service will be of benefit to that company, demographic, or industry. Using this technique will help your audience learn more about what you do and deliver more and better-qualified referrals.

Chapter 7
Getting Noticed and Being Fabulous

My boss at my first professional job at the theater called everyone "darling" and everything "fabulous." She may have been a depressed, often-intoxicated chain-smoker with a knack for saying the wrong things, but she was fabulous. This woman had the marvelous ability to turn heads with her entry into a room, smooth ruffled donor feathers, calm fiscal fears, raise millions of dollars, and be memorable (even if it wasn't always a positive kind of memorable).

I learned a lot from this remarkable woman, who once told me with complete conviction that I would thank her one

shy girl tip:
Pulling Off Fabulous

Do you know someone who is great at his or her job and exudes a fabulous charisma? Find something about this person that you can emulate and make your own—the way he or she always has a ready compliment, offers to stay late, or remembers birthdays.

day. I haven't yet, even after all this time, figured out for what exactly I was supposed to thank her (beyond giving me an interesting study of human behavior and teaching me about true workplace stress). I mostly remember her for her unique style, her interesting grip on reality, and her own overwhelming extroverted sense of self-importance.

Being fabulous—unless your chosen career is that of a drag queen—is not about being remembered for your heavy makeup, bad perfume, and gravity-defying hair. Being fabulous is about being great at what you do and having the charm and charisma to let others know how great you are without being overwhelming. As an introvert, you may shy away from the idea of being fabulous initially, but with practice and self-awareness, you can become the best kind of fabulous: the kind that is the positive kind of memorable.

Maybe I do need to thank her.

WHAT DOES YOUR BUSINESS CARD SAY ABOUT YOU?

Despite all of the advances in technology, business cards have stood the test of time. The simple tradition of passing a card with your name to someone you meet is still a staple of most business and networking meetings. Even better, a business card is another great tool for the introverted.

Have you ever taken the time to think about what your business card says about you? Have you ever looked at your card with fresh eyes to see what someone else might see when they look at your card? Your card should express who you are and what you do. Have you ever made a judgment about someone on the basis of his or her business card? Have you ever found someone else's card hard to read?

When you are out networking, you will hopefully end up with a handful of business cards. You may even eventually end up with a pile that will need to be sorted and organized. If you are serious about networking, you will look at these cards again, contact the people you have met, and build stronger relationships. At some point someone will pull out your card too. What will that person see? Will your card inspire him or her to set up a meeting with you?

Remember, just as you may not remember the details of every person you meet, some, if not most, will not remember you either. The good news is you gave them your card.

You may work for a company or organization that has already provided business cards for you—and if so, that's great, although it does seriously limit the impression your card can leave. However, if you have the opportunity to design your own cards or to work with your company to create a card that more effectively represents you and that business, then take it. Your business card says volumes about you without you having to say a word. This is a big plus for an introvert not as inclined to talk about him- or herself.

Here are some tips for developing your perfect business card:

1. Use a good-quality card stock. Nothing says "cheap and unprofessional" quite like a bad business card. Your card may be your only lasting impression. Make it worth it. You can usually purchase a box of professionally printed business cards for $40 to $100.

2. Consider using your picture. A picture is worth a thousand words. A small head shot can help jog the memory of a new contact and help them recognize you when you meet one-on-one. Make sure the picture is professional, clear, and well placed on the card.

3. Include your name and title. Your name should be big and easy to read. Name and title are the most important things on your card, and a good font size makes it easy for your card to be found among others.

4. Include the name of your business or logo. I hate to even mention this—it should be self-explanatory, but I have run into a couple cards over the years that missed this seemingly obvious inclusion.

5. Include a notation about what you do. Bullet points or a line that states what you do are of the utmost importance. Don't make it difficult for someone to remember why you are so important to call.

6. Include a tagline. Do you have a catchy tagline or memory hook? If not, think of one. This will help people remember what you do.

7. Avoid getting too fancy. Choose a font that is clear and easy to read. The old standbys like Times New Roman and Arial are my favorites and work well on business cards.

8. Include general contact information and email. This is another obvious suggestion but also is important. Double-check this vital information before sending the cards to print. Remember to have your cards reprinted if a number or address changes.

9. Include a website address. If you have a website address, include this information prominently so that additional information on your products, servicing, and pricing can be looked up at any time. If I can avoid calling or emailing someone until I know more about the business, I will. This is a courtesy to other introverts and a favor to oneself, because you will increase the likelihood of more qualified inquiries and avoid calls from people who are calling just to ask for your website address.

10. Choose your card colors carefully. Full-color cards are expensive, and they are usually not necessary. A black-and-white card is easy to read and traditional, but you can also choose blue or another dark color to make your card stand out. However, if you work in graphic arts or other visual industry, or if you have chosen to include a photo, color cards may be the way to go.

11. Consider the shape of your card. Artistic companies (such as advertising agencies) or those wishing to be perceived as edgy (like Internet companies) will sometimes choose a nonstandard shape for their business cards. Remember, while this may have the desired effect of being artistic, many people store their cards in a card file, Rolodex, or card book. If your card does not fit, it may just irritate someone enough to throw out your card. I threw out a business card the other day that looked like and was the size of a million-dollar bill. While this was a cute idea, it was an awkward size. I worried about getting it mixed in with my real money and inadvertently paying the pizza guy with the fake money. It also didn't fold in any way that I could read the contact information easily if I had slipped it into my file. I have worked with a few companies that have had two types of cards printed just for this reason. Interesting cards are interesting, but they may also backfire and be tossed out after the novelty has ended.

12. Use the other side. As long as your card has enough white space on the front, you can use the other side of your card to list your services, hours of operation, a special deal, or a coupon. Be creative; the back of the card can be used in a lot of unique and interesting ways that can help you convert and measure business.

13. Go with nonglossy. Unless you expect that all of the people you hand a card to carry around a permanent marker, don't choose glossy paper. Many people like to write notes on business cards. Make your card easy to write on, and you will increase your chances of someone remembering why they need to talk to you again. (Do you need to go glossy? Then make sure to keep the other side matte!)

Ultimately, the decisions you make about that little 3-inch piece of paper say an awful lot about you, your commitment to your business, the type of quality your customers can expect, and what kind of thought went into one of the biggest marketing decisions you will make.

CONNECTING EFFECTIVELY WITH OTHER PEOPLE

It is said, "You never get a second chance to make a first impression." We all know that first impressions are very important, but they are especially important when we network. You may have only a few seconds to positively connect with someone new. Any one new person may make a dramatic impact on you and your business. This can be especially daunting for introverts.

Meeting new people or even talking with acquaintances can be very scary. When we are particularly shy and self-conscious, we sometimes give off unconscious physical signals through body language. Body language can leave someone with a positive or horrendous impression of you, even if the exact same thing is said. Take these two examples.

EXAMPLE 1

Bob, feeling uncomfortable at a networking event, stands quietly in a corner. He keeps his eyes diverted, carefully not making eye contact with anyone. Bob's coworker Janet and another woman come up to Bob, who has just shoved his hands deep into his pockets. Janet says: "Bob, I would like to introduce you to Sally. Sally is from Medicom." Bob looks up briefly, hands still in pockets, his shoulders slumped, and he gives a barely audible: "Hi, nice to meet you, I'm Bob," before looking away from Sally and focusing on the large potted plant behind her.

EXAMPLE 2

Bob, feeling uncomfortable at a networking event, but wishing to give a good impression and meet some new people, stands quietly in a corner. He smiles at the people in the room making brief eye contact. Bob's coworker Janet and another woman come up to Bob. Bob smiles an even bigger smile, recognizing Janet, and gives the other woman a welcoming wave. Bob takes a step forward and extends his arm to shake hands. "Hi, nice to meet you, I'm Bob," he says, still smiling. Sally outstretches her hand and introduces herself.

These examples may seem extreme. But they are played out every day all over the world. Can you see what a big difference body language makes in first impressions?

Body language also tells us when to approach a stranger and how someone feels about us. We follow these signals without thinking most of the time, but have you ever considered what your body language is saying about you?

I cross my arms a lot. Usually it is because I am cold. But crossed arms are a signal that someone is guarded and not receptive. I have to be aware of my own body language to make sure I am not giving off the wrong signals. This gesture of crossed arms alone may make someone decide not to talk to you or to stop talking to you. It could make him or her guarded and uncomfortable. It may give the other person the impression that you aren't interested in what you are being told or in the person talking to you.

There are many books and online resources on body language. The following are just a few ways to attract positive attention and give off a great first impression when networking:

1. Smile. Smiling gives the impression that you are friendly, interested, approachable, and happy.

2. Don't cross your arms. Crossing arms is a protective, often-unconscious gesture that makes a person look guarded and unfriendly. If you find it difficult, it may help to hold a drink or a pen. This will give your hands something to do, and you will be less likely to fall into this bad habit.

3. Stand up straight. How many times did your mother tell you to stand up straight? Mom was right. Good posture gives the impression of confidence and makes you more physically attractive. You look more welcoming and are more likely to be positively remembered when you have good posture.

4. Don't fidget. Fidgeting hands or feet are distracting and disconcerting to others. Keep your feet firmly planted and your hands still.

5. Give a good handshake. A firm, strong handshake gives a great impression. Whenever you meet a new person, introduce yourself and extend your hand for a good handshake—every time.

6. Make eye contact. When speaking to others, keep eye contact, but be careful not to stare. To keep from staring, try looking at the whole person's face—the eyes, nose, and mouth. Move slowly from one to another while speaking and listening. Always return to the eyes anytime you are making a strong point. (Be careful not to do this too much. It may give the impression that you are flirting or that you are really, really dizzy!)

It is important to observe other people as well. You already pay attention to other people's body language to a certain degree; it is natural. But do you pay acute attention? By observing others carefully, you will realize that you are being told a lot about a person and become more in tune with your own body language.

Unless you think about it, your body language may give off the wrong impression. Think about how you are standing, what your arms and legs are doing, and your facial expressions. By being conscious about your presentation, you will draw in more people, those people will leave with a better impression of you, and you will build a stronger network.

– ACTIVITY –
OBSERVING BODY LANGUAGE

Watch the people around you. Notice how they sit, stand, and walk. How do they use their hands when they talk? What do you assume about these people solely on the basis of their body language? Can you differentiate between positive body language and negative body language in other people? How can you be more aware of your own silent signals?

DEVELOPING YOUR BUSINESS NETWORKING SKILLS

Networking is a lot like riding a bike. It takes persistence and time to learn how to network, and you may make some embarrassing spills, but once you learn how to be effective, networking will become so easy that there will be times you don't even know you are doing it. The thing to remember is that just because you have practiced networking, learned how to network, and become good at it, networking won't work unless you work at it!

The first step in polishing your networking skills is to meet with the people you already know. Do you have a coworker you talk to once in a while but aren't close with? Maybe you have friends with whom you have lost touch? Invite one of these people out to lunch or coffee and learn a little more about them.

Ask your new networking buddy how he or she has been, what he or she is up to, what interesting things he or she is doing this summer—and then listen. You will learn a lot about people, and even more about networking, just by listening. After you have spent some time learning more about this person, go ahead and tell him or her about your desire to become a better networker. These people will naturally want to help you. They may ask who you want to know, and you should know the answer to this question. Keep these meetings brief, and try to meet with one of these people once a week. You will feel more comfortable with them because you already have a relationship, you will gain practice talking to people, and best of all, you will begin to strengthen your network.

After the meeting, check his or her business card to confirm that the contact info is correct and complete in your contact management system. Remember that to maintain your relationship, you have to continue to meet with these people a few times a year, so send them that nice thank-you card and remember to call in three to four months, if not sooner, and do it again.

I met Tony, a printer, while working for a nonprofit company in Rochester, New York. My company had relationships with several printers who we used for several different promotional mailings, event brochures, and flyers. As soon as I met Tony, I liked him. He was kind, honest, and helpful. When the time came to choose where to go for a big printing project, I chose Tony to put together our fund-raising brochure.

Tony was phenomenal to work with, and the brochure turned out amazingly well and on budget. Over the next few years, through a couple of different jobs, Tony and I kept in touch. We would get together a couple of times a year just to catch up. I always enjoyed our lunch meetings; Tony knew all the best restaurants. When I started working at a web development company, I called Tony to see whether there might be interest in his company getting a new website. Tony put me in touch with the marketing manager. Although there wasn't an interest in a new website at that time, Tony and I continued to get together regularly. Eventually, through some organizational changes at his company, Tony was put in charge of marketing and given the directive to handle a website redesign. It had been six years between the time I bought brochure printing from Tony and he bought a website from me, but in the end, I not only got a new customer but also gained a friend. We shared several referrals and had several absolutely wonderful lunches, all thanks to using these networking techniques.

How do you motivate yourself to be a better networker? I sometimes need a little push out the door (or to make that phone call). Sometimes I need a goal or a challenge to get me through. Here are some suggestions to help get you going when you get stuck:

1. Set a goal. "I will make ten calls today," or "I will talk to a person today whom I've never talked to before."

2. Work with a friend. Find someone who also wants to network, and work with that person to keep yourself motivated. Challenge each other: "I can set more appointments this week than you can."

3. Create your own personal networking game. On Mondays call all of the people on your contact list whose names start with M, or set meetings with new contacts only in a certain category, like restaurants. Make it interesting or fun to get motivated.

4. Six degrees of separation. Strike up a conversation with a person you don't know well, and try to find the six degrees of separation between that person and your cousin Amy (or Bobby Joe, Fred, or George). The point is to see how you are all connected.

5. Tell someone you'll be there. By setting an appointment or agreeing to attend an event, you have made a commitment to another person. This commitment should be enough to get you there.

Whatever you need to do to get yourself out there, do it (within reason, of course). The more you network, the easier and more natural it will be, and the more successful you will be in cultivating those relationships.

TREATING YOUR LIFE LIKE A BUSINESS

By applying the same organization and discipline to your life as you do to your career, you can expect to have success in all areas of your life—work, family, home, community, friends, spirituality, and so on. Success will come because it is about more than just you—and when you broaden your view to include others, you will increase your power to positively affect all outcomes.

Introverted people sometimes put up a wall to protect from the discomfort that others often bring. Think about the times you have chosen not to consider the feelings of others over your own. In doing this, introverts forget—perhaps they never know—the joys that working for or with others can produce. Instinctually we don't bring people into our comfort zones; instead we choose to keep a private sanctuary in which to be alone. My own innate tendency as an introvert is often to put my head down and keep to myself. Sometimes it is so that I don't feel vulnerable, and sometimes it is just because I feel more at ease in this posture. It is natural to not want to open up, to take on the bulk of the responsibility, and not to bother others or seek assistance. That is, after all, what defines an introvert. Yet we use this barrier as a security blanket, and eventually this same comfort can smother us in our careers and personal lives.

Once I was able to break free of the things I thought being an introvert meant professionally, I realized I had done the same in the other areas of my life. As a businessperson I had the responsibility to do the best I could for the business and my coworkers. I escaped from the feelings that did not take the people around me into full consideration. I did whatever I could to keep customers happy, projects delivered on time, and new sales coming in. There is great success in this— but it needed to be carried out through the other aspects of my being, as it does yours. Sometimes doing this will make you stretch from your instinct, push boundaries, get more people involved, and become more involved yourself—and all of this is good.

As a professional, I work extra hard to stay organized, collaborate, make and keep connections, and lead by example. But most important, I look for opportunities to grow, teach, mentor, and delegate as appropriate. I accept constructive criticism, offer praise and rewards for a job well done, and I even use a fresh eye to look at the way my office may appear to a visitor each morning as I walk through the door. As a businessperson there is so much that I do extra well because I have chosen to take owner- ship. The same is true of you. Take ownership of yourself.

I believe that to be truly successful, you need to give all areas of your life the same attention and dedication that you give to being successful in your career. So much is made of balance, but the concept is strong. If you are going to be great in your career, it also means that you must treat the other areas of your life with the same attention. Time management, presentation, finances, organization, relation- ships, and standing with the community are all important to your ultimate success.

Take ownership of and responsibility for your life, and your job, and show the same respect to your whole life that you have dedicated to your professional life.

Chapter 8
Location, Location, Location

One personality trait that most introverts share is discomfort in new situations and new places. Having control over your environment is one way to manage your introversion in public.

When you engage in business networking with an individual or group, the choice of location is an important one, and you will often have the ability to control and influence the success of the meeting according to the location.

Given enough forethought, your comfort level, the comfort level of your guests, lighting, noise, types of seating (casual versus formal), and dress codes can all be adjusted to ensure your comfort and ultimately the success of the meeting. Think about both your ability to present yourself in the best situation and the impression you wish to convey through your surroundings.

How comfortable do you feel in different situations and settings? Do you like a casual setting or a more formal one? Part of being an introvert is that uncomfortable feeling you get when dealing with new situations and people. But you can lessen or even eliminate your anxiety and learn how to determine the location of your meetings to produce the optimal outcome.

STAGING—CREATING THE BEST ENVIRONMENT FOR YOUR PERFORMANCE

I have a theater background, but I have never been an actor. No, I never had the confidence to walk out on stage, night after night, in front of all those scary people! I think I may have secretly wanted to, but I have acted in only one real play, in a tiny little part, and it took a two-liter bottle of caffeinated soda to get my nerves and energy up enough to do so (my character was a little hyper, so it worked). While onstage I completely forgot my lines, and so I read them from the script hidden in a prop briefcase.

Instead of an actress, I became a theatrical production manager and theatrical carpenter. I was the consummate backstage tech type, right down to my construction boots and my black jeans and T-shirt. I had all the power to make things happen, yet none of the glory. It was a role that suited me quite well at the time.

Despite not specifically applying my theater degree to my career today, I do use it every day. The aspects of costume, lighting, backdrop, tone of voice, inflection, language, body language, and music are all instrumental to the way I conduct myself in my business. Even understanding how to use and trust a support team is pertinent.

I am intensely aware, when giving a presentation, of framing myself in front of something fairly plain. A plain, light-colored wall behind me will work, as long as there are no pictures on the wall or windows to draw attention away. If possible, I like to be a little higher when giving a speech or presentation, so I stand. This gives me a sense of authority and allows me to project my voice farther and more power-fully. If I want to be on par with the people I am talking to, to be part of the team, and to foster good group dynamics, I sit with the group in a circle or around a table.

I often wear red or burgundy. These power colors natu-rally suggest authority (and I have been told go well with my fair skin tone). I have also experimented with different hair colors, and when my hair is red, I get much more atten-tion and I am remembered better. Also, I don't really like to speak behind a podium; I feel that it creates a barrier between me and the group. I try to make sure the room is at a comfortable temperature and that the lighting in the room doesn't make my face look too long, short, dark, or flat. I watch for shadows that may distract the audience, and when possible, I will go to the lighting people to pick out gels to put in the lights that flatter my complexion. To calm my nerves, I hold a pen when giving a formal presentation or a cup of tea when holding a less formal meeting or one-on-one. This way I have something to do with my hands, and I don't overgesture or cross my arms.

I am a consummate control freak, but it all serves a purpose. All of these things give me control over my environment; they make me more comfortable and allow me to give the best presentation I can. My introversion is quelled by having the control of knowing that all possible success factors have been addressed. By recognizing how these factors play into what I am saying and how it is being heard, I have the power. When I have the power, I am confident. You can see how this would be beneficial!

Sometimes I am asked if I miss being in the theater. The answer is always "no" because I love what I do now, and I honestly believe that "all the world's a stage." I get to play on it every day. I play the part when necessary, and I create the reality to tell my story or share my message. When this is done well, there is no reason to be nervous about speaking; you are giving the audience exactly what you want them to see, the experience exactly as you wish them to experience it.

FINDING A COMFORTABLE HOME BASE FOR NETWORKING

There are almost as many different ways to network as there are people. You may find that you like only one type, or you may like them all, and you will find vast differences between groups, even within chapters of the same organization. So, shop around for the best fit. This will be your home base— the place that you can feel most comfortable, your own turf, to meet with the most people at once.

In general, group networking can be categorized into three types: formal, semiformal, and informal. Some types are obviously better for introverts than others, although they each have their good and bad qualities. You will excel when you are most relaxed, so find what works best for you.

Formal Networking Groups

Formal groups meet for the purpose of networking and sharing leads or referrals. Often these groups offer new friendships, support, and other important information about things going on in business or the community. These groups generally require regular attendance and dues. The benefit to a formal networking group is that you are able to build strong networks with the other members. You see the same people each week or month and get to know them well. The groups may allow only one person per industry to be a member, so there is no competition. The downside can include the time commitment, strict policies, and dues. I have found that the right formal group can make a huge difference in both my ability to increase my networking skills and the growth of my business. These groups are a great source for referral business.

Introverts will find that formal groups may be the best fit because of the structure in the agenda and the understood expectation of the attendees. There will be fewer surprises, and you will know when to speak and what you are expected to say.

Semiformal Networking Groups

The semiformal groups usually meet for educational reasons and include some sort of networking element, such as a seminar or discussion. There are many groups in this category, such as Women in Communications or the National Association of Women Business Owners (NAWBO). Alumni associations also fit into this category. These are fantastic groups, especially for networking within your industry or among your peers. The downside may include nonexclusivity in your industry and a lack of referral business because others in the group do what you do. Also, the meetings don't specifically call for referrals.

Introverts who have been networking for awhile or are a little more comfortable in social situations may enjoy a semiformal group. There will still be an agenda, a chance to learn something new, and expectations set for your participation. There will also likely be an open networking time before and or after to meet new people and chat with other participants.

Informal Networking Groups

Informal groups tend to create themselves: a mother's group, a bunch of friends that get together for coffee, and buddies from school all qualify. These types of groups provide a wonderful networking opportunity, especially if you pay attention. Your friends, family, and coworkers all have information they need and information you want. Sometimes you just need to listen harder and ask the right questions.

Informal groups are valuable because leads and referrals come naturally, and the environment is very casual. But you may also have to work to keep the group going, as attendance generally isn't required and the meetings are unstructured. Expect that not everyone in the group will have the same agenda, and don't be afraid to express your objectives for the group to keep it productive.

Introverts may feel very uncomfortable, as I do, in the informal groups. It can be unsettling to be in a room with a bunch of people and no natural, preset activity. However, if the group is familiar to you, or if you attend with an extroverted friend or colleague, you may find that the low-key atmosphere works for you.

You may choose one type or multiple types of groups. The best way to find the place for you is to visit several different types of meetings, but choose according to your interests. Many times these groups have a visitor host or greeting committee. Connect with these people immediately. I recommend that introverts like myself also bring a friend, especially an outgoing friend, to lessen the stress of meeting new people. Or consider going to a meeting with someone who is already a member and who will introduce you to the other members and answer any questions that you have.

No matter what kind of group you choose, make sure that it makes sense for you to be to there—your time is precious, so make it worthwhile. The agenda must fit your needs, and the people in the group must have similar goals and interests.

– ACTIVITY –
NETWORKING TYPES

Choose from the list below and check off the boxes that most fit with what you are looking for. Do you prefer formal or informal gatherings? Are you comfortable in groups or one-on-one? Which category or categories do you feel would have the greatest impact on you and your business?

Contact and referral networks

- Structured agenda
- Regular meeting time
- Goal of passing business referral
- Limited to one member per profession
- Formal

Service organizations

- Casual networking
- Provide and support community and humanitarian works
- Semiformal

Casual-contact networks

- Less-structured environment

- Focus on referrals and knowledge building
- Membership not limited by profession
- Semiformal

Professional associations

- Support and promote as well as exchange information within a given industry
- Members are all in the same industry or type of industry
- Semiformal

Social and business organizations

- Combine social activities with business networking
- Casual

Online networks

- A new way to connect
- Develop business relationships based on trust and your online network
- Varying degrees of formality

THE POWER OF THE ONE-ON-ONE

After several years of frustrating, uncomfortable cocktail-hour networking events with large groups of golf-talking, suited men who reminded me of my father and greasy-haired, pimply-faced, unemployed computer geeks who showed up for the free beer and who did more awkward flirting than networking, it was obvious that I needed a change of networking venue.

These pseudo-informal networking gatherings left me with feelings of failure and defeat. I lost hours of my life that I will never get back. I would build up the courage to go, and then stand in the corner, busy myself with ordering a drink, go to the bathroom to fix my hair, read the signs on the walls—anything that I could do to avoid having an actual conversation. I felt either invisible or like a rare anomaly (I was often one of very few women in attendance). If I did see someone who I knew there, I would cling to him or her like a safety net, idly and unsuccessfully trying to make small talk about the event, or the weather, or a recent technology trend. I was losing out on a great opportunity to meet new people and extend my network, and I knew it, but I couldn't bring myself to change and be more outgoing. There had to be a better way.

During this time, I belonged to several groups whose purpose was to encourage networking. I suppose I thought that the more groups I belonged to, the more people I could network with. But I wasn't really networking with anyone. I was working for a small company and responsible for making sales necessary to keep us in business. I needed to network, and I knew it.

One day, in desperation, I was looking for a little networking inspiration, and I turned to my bookshelf and picked up the membership book from the Women in

Communications group—which was organized by profession—and I devised a plan. There was a way to network on my terms. I sat down and began to email a few of the members from the book to ask them to meet with me one-on-one. I started with the business owners, and I told them a little about me and that I was looking to get advice from successful businesswomen and do a bit of networking. This started a very successful entry into real business networking and set into motion my passion for and understanding of relationship marketing.

MEETING ALL THE CEOS

I finally had a realization after all of those unsuccessful attempts at networking: I do much better one-on-one. I remember people's names, I am more relaxed, and I begin to build a relationship with the person with whom I am talking. Not to mention that I present myself better! All of the women I called to meet in the membership book were in communications—public relations, advertising, marketing, and so on. These people were my target market. I contacted each of the members in that book who were owners, presidents, or CEOs. The majority of the women were actually quite happy to meet with me. We met mostly for coffee and chatted casually. I kept the meetings as short as possible, without rushing anyone out the door, and I generally asked the same questions and told the same things about myself each time. I was rehearsed, having determined a formula for a successful meeting, improving it each time. As each meeting concluded, I felt more confident and excited about the person I had just met and interested in meeting the next person on my list. The plan was working.

I got better, and more relaxed, with each meeting. For a long time I had one meeting a day with the people in that membership book, and when the list got shorter, I moved on to other groups and organizations to which I belonged.

I was very surprised at first that so many of the members agreed to meet with me. However, now I myself will jump at the chance to sit and talk to an up-and-coming business-person who is interested in me. It is always such an honor to be asked to share my story. I hope that this is how these women felt. They made a significant contribution to my success and my ability to further my career, just by taking some time to chat.

Today, I continue to value the one-on-one meeting. I try to schedule several meetings with new people weekly and grow current relationships with contact meetings daily. When I am asked by someone to sit for a networking meeting, I make every effort to do so, because of its potential value and my understanding that asking me may have been difficult to do for an introvert. The most notable effect that this has had on my work is that I have not had to cold-call in years. The meetings, as well as being fun and interesting, produce leads, referrals, and interest in my company and in me.

It is not the amount of people you meet, but what you do with the relationships that matters, and I have cultivated these relationships into great friendships and rewarding business partnerships.

In writing this book, I have requested assistance from several people, including a well-known local philanthropist and author of a book on money management. I was delighted that she agreed to the meeting, as we had previously met only in passing. The meeting was beneficial to me because she was able to give me some excellent advice about book writing and publishing, but also because she told me that she was an introvert. I had heard this dynamic woman speak, and she is well respected in our community. I would not have initially thought that she was an introvert, and her insight and experience in managing her introversion was very helpful. I never would have had her perspective had I not stepped outside my comfort zone and asked her for a meeting, or if she had not stepped outside of her comfort zone and agreed to meet with me.

WHY I LIKE COFFEE SHOPS

I don't drink coffee, but that doesn't stop me from frequenting coffee shops. For me, coffee shops are an ideal place to meet new people and an absolute gift to the introvert. Coffee shops are relaxed, casual places. Coffee doesn't have to last long, so if the meeting isn't going well, you can always finish up your coffee (or tea, or hot chocolate, or overpriced fruit smoothie) and politely excuse yourself.

The environment is pretty standard (a couple of over-stuffed sofas and coffee tables, a few tables and chairs) so you know what to expect. You usually pay ahead of time, so you don't have to wait for the waitress to deliver a check, and most of the time, as long as you order a drink or two, they will let you sit there for hours.

I love coffee shops and the many little cafés that have popped up over the past few years. I don't care much if they are artsy or commercialized, I just look for them to be centrally located and have a nice place to sit. Many of them even have a free Internet connection, so I can stay connected with the people at work, check my email, and shoot that note off to a client. Best of all, a coffee shop is neutral ground. At coffee shops, the chairs are the same size, there is no large desk to separate us, no papers to shuffle, no clients coming in for the next meeting. I meet people at coffee shops for dozens of reasons: ease, comfort, the delicious chai latte—they just work for me. Unless your meeting is with the actual owner or manager of the coffee shop, neither you nor the other person will have a power advantage.

Not too long ago I broke my standard rule of business networking and met with a gentleman who does corporate training. As I walked in, he hurriedly took me on a tour of his building, showing off everything from the break room to the conference room. And then he ushered me into his office and immediately began to write his agenda for the meeting on his white board:

9:35–9:40—discuss corporate differentiators

9:40–9:45—business background

9:45–9:55—1 year goals

It went on like that in five-minute increments, and he scrawled additional agenda items until I couldn't take it any more and I said, "Stop—really, just sit. Let's just get to know each other."

From there a strange power struggle developed in which our different styles became exaggerated and awkward. He wanted to take control of the meeting by dictating how we would spend each of the forty-five minutes we had together, and I wanted him to sit and tell me about himself, express an interest in me and my business, and for us to develop a natural and casual connection.

He pushed back, expressing his need to show me how he conducts business—presumably by micromanaging his guests' and employees' time—and I pushed back, not wanting to be manipulated into an agenda that I did not agree to or wish to participate in.

Needless to say, it went downhill from there. Now, there are a dozen ways this could have gone better, and I sincerely wanted to give this connection a chance. As I left, I was frustrated at both me and him and how it had gone, and I mustered all I could to ask this gentlemen if we could meet up again in a couple weeks.

I think he realized the importance, as I did, of finding common ground with each other. It is not always true that the people you network with will be ones that you keep connected with; however, in this case we had similar contacts and mutual business. He agreed to meet again two weeks later.

Thankfully, he was amenable to a meeting at a local café for breakfast. That morning I arrived early and scoped out a good seat by the door so that I could watch him come in. I was apprehensive and awaited his arrival nervously. As he came to the table, he was relaxed, smiled, and shook my hand. We had a delightful breakfast and talked easily about the arts, traveling, and our businesses. It was a much appreciated and profound change from the previous meeting.

By taking the meeting to a neutral place, we were able to be peers. By choosing a venue that I was familiar with and a predetermined and nonbusiness activity (eating), I was able to be comfortable, and we were able to have a casual discussion. It was actually very nice—and in the end I felt much better about the gentlemen—and his company.

By changing the location of the meeting, we changed the outcome. I knew I was more at ease in a more neutral setting, and in the end, this is where we should have met in the first place.

Meeting new people away from my office where I can be interrupted or in their office where they can be interrupted, or even where they may feel compelled to take control, is a strategy to manage my introversion and be able to focus my attention fully on the meeting.

Coffee shops may not work for you. You might like to meet people in your office or theirs, out for lunch, or someplace else. The point is that to manage being timid, shy, or introverted, you must begin to feel comfortable.

Chapter 9
Organization

Being organized seems like a pretty natural quality for a successful businessperson, introverted or not, but what if you aren't a color-coding, label-maker-loving, list-creating, designer-file-color kind of person? Are you doomed to fail?

No.

However, to keep track of all of your new contacts and ensure that you follow up in a timely manner, you will need to find an organizational method that works for you. If you have never made a priority of keeping a contact list—let alone one for the purposes of networking—then now is the time to start.

The thing with organization is that if you are the kind of person who piles, then pile. If you are the type of person that files, then file. Find a system and go with it. There are enough products on the market for any style and budget to keep you in check—that is, if you are able to stick with a system. And that is where I have a problem.

If you are like me, you prefer filing but fall into dropping everything at the front door or kitchen table when you walk in the house and then shove it into a corner when cleaning up. The same happens to my computer files, which all get dumped into a "Meg" file on my desktop.

Organizing is fun for me when I get the chance to do it. All too often, though, I don't feel like there is enough time. As with so many other things, the time it takes to do it right and maintain it is far less than the time wasted trying to find a file or paper, over and over again, in a continually frustrating daily cycle that is the source of profound consternation and disheartenment.

I have enlisted the help of my good friend Stacy on many occasions to help me organize. She truly (obsessively) loves organizing, and for the record is a true extrovert, so sharing her time and ideas comes naturally for her. She is able to get me to sit down and put things in order. Then when I feel myself slip, I just think about how she is going to give me a hard time if she ever sees it in such a state again. (I picture her knocking on my door, fists full of highlighters, paper clips, and sticky notes!)

For me, having Stacy come and help me organize is less about her organizing skills (although she is undeniably the most organized person on the planet); it is about being accountable to someone else. I invite my friend over, we are obligated to work on the project, I get the stuff out, we go through it, and it takes a fraction of the time it took to actually find the time to make the invite, schedule the meeting, and actually get together. As a bonus, I get to spend time with my friend and enjoy a nice cup of tea. (Oh yeah, and my stuff is organized!)

Organization is about efficiency, and efficiency is another way you can stand out from the crowd no matter how shy or introverted you are. You will be able to accomplish what needs to be done in less time, and in doing so, devote those valuable moments you gain back to the things that matter most.

– ACTIVITY –
START GETTING ORGANIZED

Make a list of all the things that you would like to organize. Don't be afraid to think about work and home stuff; they both relate to the efficiency (and inefficiency) of your life.

Here are some ideas:
- Files
- Business goals
- Personal goals
- Calendar

- Tax paperwork
- Contact list
- Email
- Bills
- Pantry
- Housework
- To-dos

Take your list and then prioritize. Do the organizing of each of these areas in the order of importance, considering first the activities that have the greatest impact on your ability to do your job to the best of your ability. Do not move on to the next item on the list until you have completed the task at hand. By breaking these up, you will be able to accomplish the smaller goals and stay focused. Now get started!

HANDLING BUSINESS CARD OVERLOAD

As you begin the process of becoming a Master Networker (see chapter 11), you may find that you too will start piling the business cards on your desk. So how do you remember all of those people you will meet? And how will you find a way to sort through all of those cards?

I was recently asked how I manage the dozens of business cards that I can acquire at any given event—and I realized that over time, I have developed a very sophisticated system. Business cards are super tools, but you have to know how to use that tool to make it effective. Otherwise, you are just collecting a lot of useless paper. If I am at an event, I am often internally a bit flustered. I miss details and have trouble remembering names and faces because my introversion has me tangled up in thoughts of when I might get to leave or where I may be able to hide out until the event is over. Of course, I make an effort to fight the internal battle; however, my memory of each person I meet usually fails. With business cards, I can not only give a new contact my information but also help my memory—and increase my potential for getting to know that person better later.

LEAVING YOUR MARK

The first thing I do when I get a business card (or soon after) is to make a note of the date and event where I met the person. This not only gives me something to do as I stand there awkwardly but also gives me a reference point later on. If we talk about something interesting, I will write that down too. (For example, I write: "BNI 10/15/04, looking for partnership w/ software co.") If there is anyone that I want to get together with again right away or send a card or email to, I put a little asterisk in the corner. Some people get a lot of notes; others do not. It all depends on the length of the conversation and the points I feel are necessary to remember later on.

This technique will help you to identify a new contact after some time has passed, but also the ritual of making note of the most basic details of your meeting will create an instant connection with the person you just met. The connection made by putting that pen to paper solidifies your brain's ability to remember that new person.

You may find that the note is not even necessary later on to remind you, but believe me—it is important to get into the habit. It will save you a lot of frustration and lost opportunities later on. It also is a great way to find someone at a restaurant or coffee shop if you have set up a meeting. If you know you are looking for a woman with short hair in her fifties with glasses, you will have a much easier time finding the right table and appearing like you have a great memory (even if you don't!).

CARD FILING AND FILING THE CARDS

Occasionally falling prey to the mentality of out of sight, out of mind, I keep a box to drop business cards into when I get home. About once a week, I go through the box and pull out the cards of the people with whom I would like to network. At this point I also go through my contact wish list to see whether there is an opportunity to meet with any of these people as well or to see whether any of my contacts would benefit from meeting each other. Different needs come up at different times, and a card might stay in that box for a while, so I group them by "urgent" (the people I met that I want to meet with immediately) and then by industry: accounting, banking, cable, landscaping, mortgage, phone, software, and so on. I email them each a little note. For example, "It was great to chat with you at the event last week. I would love to get together sometime for coffee and see if there is a way our businesses could work together."

Then those cards get entered in my contact management database. (I learned long ago that it was just plain silly to enter every card I ever got. I focus on the ones that make sense to contact.) By putting this system in place, I have incorporated this process into my job. This makes procrastinating less likely and makes it easier to make that call or send the email. My introversion is overridden by my need to follow my system and keep the process in place, and because I write them a note, I know that in the future I will have already made a solid connection, so calling them later will seem much less intimidating.

MOVIN' ON UP

After meeting with a contact for a second time, I will make a note in the database about the meeting, the date, the place, and so on. And I send the person an old-fashioned card thanking him or her for taking the time.

If the person and I are able to find a mutually beneficial business relationship, then the card is moved into the card file. I use a three-ring binder for my cards because I can see multiple cards at once, and I can bring that binder with me from my home office to the work office. I organize by industry and by last name—it is very effective. If that person becomes a frequent and beneficial contact, they are moved up to the front of the binder, where I keep the most important contacts.

GETTING ON THE LIST

I have one final card management system: my book. In my contact book are my key or A-list contacts. My A-list includes my contacts from my networking groups, and I usually have multiple cards for each contact. I use the book to help out the people I meet and my key contacts. You never know when you might be talking to someone who mentions that he or she wants to put an addition on the house in the spring or needs a new computer or needs to send a gift basket to a client. Networking is not just about meeting new people for you; it is about creating a network of people who work together. I may be able to help a new contact by putting him or her in touch with someone who can help out or who might be interested in that person's product. I build goodwill, establish myself as helpful and connected, and give my new contact a reason to remember me the next time that he or she hears about someone in need of a website.

Using a similar system will help get you organized, naturally motivate you to connect with those contacts, and further increase your aptitude as a Master Networker!

NETWORKING GOLD—YOUR LIST

Your list is made up of your network contacts. This list is the most valuable part of business networking. It never ceases to amaze me how we mistreat our lists and, ultimately, those in our networks. Meeting new people is not enough; you must develop a system to maintain this list.

Do you keep a list now? Do you keep a list, database, or address book for your friends and family?

Some businesspeople don't even keep an actual list. In fact, many small businesses don't keep lists, and those that do rarely keep them up to date. If you can keep your list of business contacts just in your head, you are not and will not be doing enough business to sustain yourself in the long term. Vendors, clients, partners, friends, prospects, potential vendors, and potential partners all should be included in your network! You should be contacting these people in some way or another at least once every ninety days. If you do not contact them regularly, they will probably not remember you when and if you do call, and therefore they aren't really in your network. Also, remember that it is always easier to call on someone you know than on someone you don't. By maintaining these strong relationships, you can avoid the frustration of always trying to establish new networks.

WHERE IS THAT CARD?

I have a friend—a CEO of a technology company—who keeps his important contacts' business cards rubber banded in piles on his desk. He must believe that having a business card for a contact is all he needs. Or maybe he doesn't think he has the time to sort through them. There are probably six or seven 4-inch piles on his desk right now. Is this any way to treat the people most important to your business success? How much time do you think my friend spends going through his cards to find the one phone number he is looking for on any given day? How many potential clients never get a call back?

Leaving piles of business cards on one's desk is actually a very common but unfortunate organizational method. Perhaps it is even one you have employed. Just for fun, next time you visit a business, check the desks. You will see it over and over again. This it is not very effective, and just think how many times your business card landed in the piles on the desk of a prospect or potential vendor. How does it make you feel to think your card is sitting in a pile with hundreds of other cards? Not very special. It is necessary to treat your business card collection with the respect that your contacts deserve.

SHOULD I PUT THAT IN A DATABASE?

It may be important to save the actual cards for several reasons, but it is also recommended that your contacts be typed into a spreadsheet or database. Sorting by category, location, mail merge, alphabetically, and importance is critical to managing your network. Remember that managing your network is part of your job—no matter what your official title is!

Computer technology has made the task of managing your contacts extremely easy. The average person can usually get away with just typing the information into a spreadsheet, but database systems exist that make things easier for more elaborate lists and requirements.

Below are the top five reasons that you need to take the time to do this:

1. Pure organization. Without it, it is very likely that you will forget who your contacts even are. Once the information is in a spreadsheet, it can be sorted and reports can be made easily. Then you might have to go and meet someone again—and there is nothing worse for an introvert than that!

2. Correspondence. Sending out regular correspondence, via card, letter, newsletter, email, or other direct mail is critical, not only to stay in touch but also to create new business. The spreadsheet will make this incredibly easy. Bulk email or newsletters are a cinch, and pulling up an address in a time crunch is a wonderful thing.

3. Value to your company. Your value to a lot of people, including your employer, may be in whom you know. Maintaining the list will quickly show how many and what kinds of people are in your network, and it shows that you take building the business seriously.

4. Value to your other contacts. With your contacts neatly typed into a spreadsheet, it is easy for you to make a referral. Should you be asked for a referral for a computer hardware company, a plumber, or an orthodontist, the information is easily retrievable, sorted, and printed out. You are a resource to your contacts, and the value in that is immeasurable.

5. You will only need to type it once. Should you want to create a tracking report to track when you last contacted the people on your list, to create a list for calls, or decide to integrate the list into a database, the information is already there. You will save time—time you can spend making more contacts!

RESPECT THAT LIST

Your contact list is a powerful tool. Respect it.

As an introvert, it may be quite an accomplishment to overcome your shyness and learn ways to make these connections, and over time, you should have quite a collection of contacts. But it is important that once you get the list together, you regularly go through it to purge. No matter how many new contacts you make, your list will get stale without regular care, and you cannot rely on the connections you made last year to carry you through next year without attention. You should also

---

shy girl tip:
Alone Time

One of the best parts of organizing your list is that it is one of the few activities that truly can be done alone. Remember that it is very important to allow yourself the time to recharge, and while the process of updating and purging your list is very important, so is the time spent enjoying solitude!

clean out your business card file when you do this. Over many months or years, your contacts will move, change jobs, change numbers, or even change jobs within a company. Sometimes you will just know this information in your head, which is terrific—until you send out your Christmas cards with a mail merge from your list and end up having half the cards sent back, or more embarrassing, have the cards get to the right company but not the right contact person.

The key to keeping a good networking list is to keep it limited to only people that you truly know. Networking is not a contest to see how many business cards you can collect. Go ahead and enter every person you meet and their information into a second list or database if you like, and send them a newsletter or an email blast. But those people are still not your network until you hear back from them. It is likely that you won't even know half of them in six months. Networking is about building quality, long-term relationships. It is better to have a smaller, closer group than a larger group of people who don't know who you are. I have about three hundred people in my network—and perhaps two thousand names in my database of people I have met and with whom I made some sort of connection. The difference is that I work extra hard to maintain my network. The large database of contacts is useful for email blasts or direct mail about company news, but it never gets the same return as my network mailings. You can always move these people into your network later on, but networking is work. It won't happen unless you are an active participant.

THE A-LIST AND THE B-LIST

Once your contact base and list begins to grow, it is important to further separate your contacts into your A-list and B-list. The A-list should consist of the approximately fifty people with whom you do the most business, give the most referrals to, and/or get the most referrals from. They can be top clients, close friends, and associates. This list needs to be tended even more carefully than your regular network (or B-list), because there may be a fair amount of turnover from A-list to B-list. As people move, change jobs, and so on, they will become more or less important to your network. Don't be afraid to move them around or remove them entirely.

A-list contacts should be met with, or spoken with by phone, at least once a month (and if they are clients, probably even more frequently, depending on your business). Email, while a nice way to stay in touch casually, does not replace the personal touch that your A-list people require. They should also be included in any bulk communication you send to the main list, but they need to be taken care of, above and beyond your typical contacts. These are the people you take out to coffee or lunch or call just because.

Your time will be well spent maintaining your list, and it will save you countless hours in the long run. Remember to treat your list and the people on it with the utmost respect. Keep your list up to date, think of these people often, and offer as much assistance to them as possible. These people will be there for you if you are there for them.

Networking is not about selling. Networking is about growing and maintaining relationships. It is the single most important way for an introvert to make connections. Do not try to sell something when you meet people to network. They may not want to meet with you again. By being yourself, friendly, engaging, and interesting, your network will naturally seek you out when they are ready to make a decision regarding buying your product or service.

Chapter 10
Your Communication Toolbox

Being a good communicator is essential to your success. There are far too many examples in my life, and I am sure in your life as well, where poor communication was the cause of an unfortunate or disappointing situation.

Everyone has a virtual communication toolbox in which little bits of conversation starters (and movers) exist. In this toolbox are also the tools that will aid you in communicating in any situation that arises. It is important for the introvert who may be tongue-tied or nervous in social situations to be able to pull from this metaphorical box and get through the sticky conversations with an interesting question, a bit of trivia, or a clever quip.

Johnny Carson hosted the *Tonight Show* from 1962 to 1992, and each night Johnny would deliver a brilliant and funny monologue. However, a committee of writers wrote these monologues, and on several occasions a joke would just fail miserably. The crowd was often unforgiving, firing back a chorus of groans and boos. Johnny's grace, wit, and quick humor in getting through these situations became one of his signatures, and he is an inspiration to us introverts who sometimes get caught in one of those "Uh-oh, everyone's watching me, and I have just said something really stupid" moments. Johnny had his toolbox full of funny gestures, facial expressions, and one-liners.

Fill your toolbox with your elevator speech, a quick biography of yourself, your company's unique value proposition, and a few interesting (but not too personal) stories that you can pull out when you meet someone who wants to know more about you, and a few general-consumption jokes if you have the ability to deliver them (I can't deliver a joke to save my life). The box should also contain the traditional interview-type responses: What was your most challenging experience? How did you overcome adversity? What are your strongest skills? Practice these and think about other tidbits of information that you would like to add. Do not be afraid to subtly acknowledge in these prepared responses that you are good at what you do and an interesting person to know.

One of the things that I will do when I am at a loss for something to say to someone is ask, "Are you doing something fun this weekend?" This elicits a variety of responses and is a little more original than, "Nice weather we're having." I listen to the reply, and I'm able to learn a little more about the person with whom I am speaking. This helps me make a connection, and it gives us something to talk about without putting any pressure on the conversation.

One of the scariest things for an introvert is telling people about themselves. We fear judgment and rejection. Put some thought into responses and conversation starters in your toolbox, keep the box full and up-to-date, and you won't have to ever worry about what you are going to say if you get stuck. Once the conversation gets started, you will be able to continue, without fear and with confidence.

MANAGING YOUR NETWORK

Managing your network begins with managing your contacts, but there is a lot more that must be done to be successful. To have a quality network, you need to engage these people, keep them informed, assist them when possible, and remember to request assistance from them when needed.

Your network will not exist without proper management. As with any responsibility, this is work, and it has to be taken seriously. Now that you have put your contacts in order, developed or purchased a good customer relation-ship management system, and built a base for your network, the real work begins.

To review, here is the number-one principle for managing your network: stay in touch.

I cannot stress the importance of regular contact with people (all of the positive people in your life) enough. Be creative by sending articles and company newsletters; invite members out to lunch, golf, and so on. Send personal notes, letters, and cards. Offer to help with their charity events or special projects. Introverts don't often have the desire or luxury of making new friends and contacts at every turn; we do, however, have the potential to make these relationships strong. Your network is your lifeline, and the quality of this network is directly proportional to the kind of success you will have.

That's it! Staying in touch is the most important thing to remember about making your network work for you.

STAYING IN TOUCH

Thirty Minutes a Day

You have an A-list and a B-list, you have your database, and you have practiced and become comfortable networking. You have a million things to do, and you have to stay in touch with all of those new contacts.

Remember that staying in touch is just as important as selling yourself, your business, or your product because your contacts are your connection with new prospects. Here is a good formula, and it only takes thirty minutes a day. Each day send five emails or make five calls and send at least two cards or letters (thank-you cards from the previous day's meetings or follow-ups with people who said they might have referrals for you). That is thirty-five connections that you made per week, and with this you will be able to set five meetings a week with new contacts and five meetings a week with current contacts as long as you stay in touch.

Once a Month

Each month, you should find a way to reach every person on your A-list again. Also, contact people who you know are having a special event this month (such as a birthday, anniversary, move, or new job). You can send them out a newsletter, card, or phone call. The purpose is to stay in touch and stay at the top of their minds.

"What do I say?" you ask. Tell them about a fund-raising event you are attending or a new product you are launching. Keep it simple. Don't try to sell. A form newsletter or email is fine for this, as long as you have sent something personal within the last month.

Chapter 11
Tips for Being a Master Networker

The fact is that it is getting more difficult to succeed personally and professionally without developing a diverse range of connections with other people. This is why becoming masterful at networking needs to be one of your main objectives, regardless of how difficult you find it to be. Remember that what you know is important, but it is not as important as who knows what you know. To be the most successful businessperson you can be, you have to overcome some of your introversion to become a Master Networker.

Being a Master Networker requires visibility, and this can be painful for the introvert who would rather focus on the job than on the relationships that surround the work. However, the two go hand in hand. One cannot succeed without the other. The good news is that you can learn the skills necessary to be a Master Networker.

Here are ten tips for being a Master Networker:

1. Do bother. Do not make the assumption that you are annoying people. Introverts will sometimes think that others do not want to be bothered (probably because we feel like we are being bothered sometimes). But don't be too quick to avoid making new contacts. Most people will be glad to hear from you.

2. Rely on your support team. Networking is challenging and will sometimes not render the results that you would like as quickly as you would like. Rely on your network of emotional supporters for empathy, encouragement, and a dose of tough love when you slack off.

3. Be a leader. Take advantage of any leadership position you are in to extend your circle of influence. Leadership roles have a built-in excuse to talk to new people and make new connections.

4. Listen. Most extroverts—OK, all extroverts—love to have people listen to them. So listen up! Become engaged in conversations, learn, ask questions, and take advantage of the fact that other people will do a lot of the networking work for you if you make yourself available and open yourself up to the relationship.

5. Go with a purpose. If you are uncomfortable and nervous at networking events, attend events such as seminars or workshops instead. These types of events have a nonnetworking agenda but still offer the opportunity to connect with others in a structured environment.

6. Reach out. If you find yourself uncomfortable in a group situation, you aren't alone. Look for other people who seem out of their element too. They will likely be grateful for a low-key, interesting person to talk to, and you will gain confidence from talking to new, easy-to-relate-to people.

7. Write. A letter of introduction, a thank-you note, or an email can be an easy way to break the ice and establish yourself as a person of manners and integrity. Make special note of birthdays, anniversaries, children's names, and interests, and be sure to send a card or use this as an opportunity to make a phone call.

8. Share. Introverts who like to read are more likely to be up on industry news and alternative communication technologies. Be the person who others call or email for information, and be sure to mail out articles of interest to your contacts.

9. Practice makes perfect. If you tend to get tongue-tied or babble on and on in tough social situations, practice with a few interesting topics ahead of time. For example, if someone five years ago asked what I did, I used to tell him or her that I was the vice president of a web development company. I'd say, "I handle business development. We do website design and development, search engine optimization, IT services, and website hosting." Polish your own elevator speech and a couple of other snippets, and you will be on your way!

10. The small stuff. Remember to connect with others on small topics as well as the big stuff. Don't wait to call or set a meeting; do it now. Reaching out just to catch up or to share some good news is a marvelous way to stay in touch and remain in the loop.

YOU ARE A GOODWILL AMBASSADOR

One of the most important aspects of networking is to be what I like to call a goodwill ambassador. As a well-connected individual, you are a tremendous resource to those around you. And being a resource will strengthen your network and ultimately your business.

Have you ever been asked whether you knew a good restaurant, dentist, contractor, bookkeeper, computer repair person, or car dealer? We are all called on at various times to provide our friends, family, coworkers, and contacts with valuable information. And the more you are considered an expert in who's who, the more you will be asked to provide this information.

My favorite goodwill ambassador calls are the ones I get from the local media. Every so often, the phone rings and I get to hear those beautiful words: "Hi, Meg, I am hoping you can help me because I know you know who I should talk to." Those calls are like gold! I get to refer a friend, client, or contact and get them publicity. I am able to be a resource for the media, and I am recognized as being someone who knows who to talk to.

Your job as a good networker is to maintain your contacts, not just for your own benefit but also for the benefit of the members in your network and the people with whom you would like to build a stronger relationship.

IT IS WHO YOU KNOW

A longtime friend asked me recently where he should go for dinner. It was a loaded question, I was sure, and after a couple carefully targeted questions, I got the whole story.

My friend was going to propose to his girlfriend, and my dear old friend (never one for living life without a bit of challenge) wanted reservations at a nice restaurant. He also wanted a private table, personal assistance from the staff in choreographing the proposal, and to propose at the restaurant the next day (a Saturday night!). And of course, he wanted my help pulling it off.

I am used to Erik being a little bit of a procrastinator; however, this was a very tall order. It was not, however, a difficult request to fulfill, because I know an exceptional restaurant and an incredible restaurant owner! I told Erik to try to make a reservation at one of my favorite local restaurants. I gave him the number and told him to tell Ellie (the owner) that he was a friend and that I had recommended they go there. Now, I knew that the restaurant would be booked on a weekend night—they always were—but Ellie was a friend, a client, and Erik's best chance at producing the perfect proposal. As I got off the phone, I smiled. I was able to help out a friend, and with any luck, Erik would be engaged by the end of the next day.

Two days later I received another call from Erik. He was ecstatic, still on a high from the proposal. He thanked me profusely for the referral and told me that Ellie had found a nice private table for him. He also said that Ellie made a point of coming over and giving them plenty of attention during dinner, had arranged for Erik's proposal to be special, and when the question was popped, the whole restaurant held their collective breath along with Erik and then erupted in a chorus of hearty applause when she said yes.

I was able to be instrumental in a life-changing, happy moment for my friend through my network. This kind of connection among people is beneficial all the way around. I was so pleased to have been able to play a part in this memory for my very good friend. And I was also happy for Ellie—what restaurant owner wouldn't want a romantic proposal on a busy night? Furthermore, Erik and his new bride will tell their story hundreds of times throughout their lives and return to the restaurant frequently, reliving one of the happiest evenings of their lives.

And for me—I received the gift of satisfaction, of fulfilling a friend's dream, of bringing business to a client, and of helping to build further business for the restaurant. But best of all, I was able to further build my confidence in my network, which motivated me to make more recommendations to others who asked for my assistance.

Life is about more than getting that sale or earning more money; it is being able to positively affect the lives of the people who are special in your life. You will be a great networker when you are able to make the connections with people like I did with Ellie and Erik, and be able to do that frequently, without hesitation.

PARTY MENTALITY—WORKING THE ROOM LIKE AN EXTROVERT

One of the best pieces of advice I ever got about networking was to treat every event like you are the host. When we hold a party, we instinctively behave like a host should, introducing people to each other, making pleasant conversation, and being sure that we spend enough time with each person at the party.

I know all too well that as an introvert it is much easier not to introduce myself to all of those people—but it will not help you build your network unless you extend your hand and say a friendly, "Hello!" So try acting like a host or the greeting committee at that next event. Offer to greet people when they arrive, or stand near the door, positioned to welcome newcomers. It is a natural location for you to introduce yourself and meet the most people, and it establishes you as a friendly face and person of interest to the other attendees. Introduce the new arrivals to someone else in the room whom they might enjoy talking to or engage them in conversation yourself.

This simple technique takes the anxiety out of meeting new people and gives you a responsibility. Take full advantage of this method, receiving business cards and following up with the people who may be of interest to you.

FRIENDS AND CONTACTS

As you collect contacts and manage your network, you will likely believe that you now have more friends than ever before—and you very well may. However, it is important to keep in mind that even though someone is a good contact, one with whom you may meet for lunch regularly or share an occasional touching moment, they are not necessarily your friend.

As an introvert, I have never had a lot of true friends. In the past ten years or so, I have collected many contacts but still have only a handful of real friends. The friends I have, I cling to, demand attention from, and hold close. At several points in my life I have changed careers; gone through personal crises; and had countless really, really bad days. The friends are the ones I call or email, the ones with whom I let my guard down, and the ones who know the real, vulnerable me. My friends are the ones that have helped me through the tough times.

I can tell the difference between the real friends and the contacts, because those people that are just contacts never meet the vulnerable, nonprofessional, timid, weak, scared me. They only know the confident, go-getter, optimistic me. These are the people who don't believe I am an introvert at all.

Who your friends are and who your contacts are becomes even more complicated when the lines begin to blur, when the friends also become business associates, coworkers, or clients.

When I decided to leave a job I truly loved, but one that I had to leave for various professional reasons, I wanted so badly to tell my friends, explain why, cry with them, and be comforted. But many of those friends had also become clients over the years and great professional contacts. I hesitated to tell them anything, because I did not want it to negatively affect their relationships with my former company and coworkers.

And that is when you find out who your friends are. Your friends are the ones you decide to talk to and the ones who care about you before themselves. They are the ones who don't say, "But who will take care of my account?" They are the ones who know that these details will be handled when the time is right and trust that you will take care of it professionally. After all, that is what made you a good friend and a good businessperson in the first place.

Keep a special place of honor for your true friends. They may be the best clients and the best contacts, but when times are tough, their ability to be great friends is what sets them apart and makes them more valuable than your entire network.

Chapter 12
Getting Away

As I finish up the writing of this book, I am reminded of one of the most important things about being aware of my needs as an introvert—sometimes I just need to get away. I repeatedly forget to take time for myself and to be alone. No matter how much socializing and public speaking and selling and being out there I do, sometimes I still just need to get away.

For me, the most refreshing, uplifting, life-affirming, healing time is spent on a quiet vacation away from the phone and work and people. I need time away from clients, coworkers, and contacts (family and loved ones generally excluded). I don't need to seclude myself on a desert island, though. Instead, I need to spend time where I do not need to interact with others unless I feel compelled to do so.

I sit here on the porch of my family cottage on Cayuga Lake in New York. The sun is shining, the water is calm, and the only noise around me is from a family of ducks and the chatter of my young son, currently tottering around preoccupied with a sippy cup of apple juice and a book he is reading upside down.

It is so easy to be caught up in the bustle, the race to succeed, and the need to break out of our shells, that we often forget that as people—and more so as introverted people—we need time to recharge, regroup, and refocus.

Be true to yourself and your

> ## shy girl tip:
> ### Recharge
>
> Take the fifteen or twenty minutes after your commute or lunch hour to take a mini-vacation. Pull into a parking spot and turn off the car. Take this time to reflect or meditate about the successes of the day. Enjoy the time alone and recharge before facing the hustle and bustle of your day.

needs. Keep in mind the importance of quiet solitude and reflection. Success in life and business comes from recognizing how you fit in, how you contribute, and when to take a step back to enjoy the view.

THE ROAD LESS TRAVELED

The truth is that there aren't that many people in the world who are truly happy or feel successful. Most of us wander through life lost without purpose or direction. This is a most profoundly distressing reality. And yet, you have the opportunity to meet the challenge and have no reason not to succeed. You have the tools, the drive, the passion, and the intelligence to make it work. Find a target and get moving.

It is impossible to write a conclusion for this book, because there is no end to the amount of success you may be able to achieve. Success and happiness are what we all want. How we go about getting there is up to us. Which path, how, why, under what circumstances, and what obstacles you have to overcome are up to you—you have the power to do and be whatever you set your mind to. So go, get out there, and do it!

Suggested Reading

Covey, Stephen R. *The 7 Habits of Highly Effective People: Powerful Lessons in Personal Change.* New York: Simon & Schuster, 1989.

Helgoe, Laurie. *Introvert Power: Why Your Inner Life Is Your Inner Strength.* Chicago: Sourcebooks, 2008.

Laney, Marti Olsen. *The Introvert Advantage: How to Thrive in an Extrovert World.* New York: Workman Publishers, 2002.

MacKay, Harvey. *Dig Your Well Before You're Thirsty: The Only Networking Book You'll Ever Need.* New York: Doubleday, 1997.

Misner, Ivan R., and Don Morgan. *Masters of Networking: Building Relationships for Your Pocketbook and Soul.* Atlanta: Bard Press, 2000.

Misner, Ivan R., and Jeff Morris. *Givers Gain: The BNI Story.* California: Paradigm Publishing, 2004.

Raelin, Joseph A. *Creating Leaderful Organizations: How to Bring out Leadership in Everyone.* San Francisco: Berrett-Koehler Publishers, 2003.

RoAne, Susan. *The Secrets of Savvy Networking: How to Make the Best Connections—for Business and Personal Success.* New York: Warner Books, 1993.

About the Author

Throughout her diverse career, Meghan Wier has been a carpenter, a special events coordinator, a professional fundraiser, a corporate relations director, a salesperson, and a vice president at businesses and organizations large and small. Ms. Wier is known for melding her professional style, keen business sense, and desire to share her work and life experiences with others. An introvert/forced extrovert, her relationship-building savvy and strong marketing skills have made her a recognized expert in building through networking. Ms. Wier is an influential authority on business networking and marketing, and she believes in the importance of managing your job as if you owned the company.

Currently, Meghan Wier is working as a writer in Charlotte, North Carolina, where she lives with her husband Jason and son Nathaniel.